Effective Test Management:

A Guide For Aspiring Test

Managers

CHAPTER 1:

INTRODUCTION TO TEST

MANAGEMENT

Over the past ten years, I've learned first-hand that being a Test Manager is as much about people and processes as it is about technology. It's a critical role at the junction of software quality assurance, team leadership, and strategic management.

In essence, a Test Manager is responsible for ensuring that a software product meets the highest quality standards before it reaches the end-user. However, that's a simplistic view. A Test Manager, in my experience, is a strategic planner, a problem solver, a leader, and a communicator. We are tasked with devising and implementing robust testing strategies, managing resources, and leading a team of dedicated testers to effectively identify and resolve issues within the software. All of these are performed while working in tandem with various other stakeholders to ensure alignment with the overall project vision.

A significant part of our job involves facilitating seamless communication across different levels and units in an organisation. Be it explaining complex testing methodologies to non-technical stakeholders or giving constructive feedback to the testing team, a Test Manager must be adept at communicating effectively.

Furthermore, we also need to be excellent negotiators, managing conflicting priorities and facilitating agreement between different stakeholders.

In my decade-long journey, I've seen the landscape of test management undergo significant transformations. With the rapid technological advancements and the proliferation of agile and DevOps methodologies, the role of a Test Manager has evolved and expanded. Today's Test Managers must have a good understanding of various testing technologies, including automation tools and AI, and be able to leverage them to optimise testing processes. At the same time, they need to be agile, being able to adapt to fast-paced, continuous development and deployment environments.

Additionally, we've seen a growing recognition of the critical role that testing plays in software development. Testing is no longer seen as a standalone activity performed after the development phase, but an integral part of the entire development process. This has placed increased responsibility on Test Managers to ensure quality across all stages of software development and foster a culture of quality within their teams and the broader organisation.

However, despite these changes and challenges, one thing has remained constant: the core objective of test management. As Test Managers, our ultimate goal is to safeguard the end-user experience. It's our responsibility to ensure that the software not only functions as intended but also meets the users' needs and expectations.

In the following chapters, I will share with you the knowledge, insights, and lessons I've gained from my experience as a Test Manager. We'll delve into the key aspects of test management, from setting up a testing team and devising a testing strategy to managing testing processes and dealing with common challenges. I hope this book will serve as a practical guide to those aspiring to be successful Test Managers in this dynamic and exciting field.

Chapter 1.1: The Role of a Test Manager

From my experience, I can tell you that the role of a Test Manager is multifaceted and challenging. It requires a unique blend of technical expertise, strategic foresight, managerial prowess, and excellent communication skills.

A Test Manager sits at the intersection of software quality, project management, and people leadership. Our primary responsibility is to ensure the software product's quality, but achieving this requires a lot more than just overseeing test executions.

From a technical standpoint, we devise and implement testing strategies that address all aspects of software quality - functionality, performance, usability, security, and compatibility, among others. It's our job to determine what needs to be tested, how it should be tested, and when it should be tested. This involves selecting suitable testing methodologies, choosing the right testing tools, and defining appropriate test metrics.

Strategically, a Test Manager plays a critical role in project planning and risk management. We contribute to project plans, estimating the time, resources, and budget needed for testing. We identify potential risks and issues that could affect software quality and devise strategies to mitigate them. It's about forecasting problems before they occur and having a plan to navigate them.

As leaders, we build and manage the testing team. This involves not just hiring and training testers, but also fostering a collaborative and positive team environment. It's our responsibility to ensure that our team members have the necessary skills and resources to perform their tasks effectively. We also need to constantly motivate and support our team, helping them overcome challenges and achieve their best.

Lastly, but most importantly, Test Managers act as the bridge between the testing team and the rest of the stakeholders. We coordinate with developers, business analysts, project managers, and sometimes even clients, to ensure everyone is aligned towards the common goal of delivering a high-quality product. We communicate test results, progress updates, and issues to stakeholders, making sure they have a clear and accurate understanding of the product's quality status. This often requires us to translate complex technical information into a language that non-technical stakeholders can understand.

Over the years, I've come to realise that being a Test Manager is not just about managing tests; it's about managing quality. It's about instilling a quality-first mindset in the team, ensuring that quality is considered at every stage of the software development process. It's about driving continuous improvement, always looking for ways to optimise testing processes and enhance product quality.

In the end, our role as Test Managers is to safeguard the interests of the end-user. We strive to ensure that the software not only meets the functional requirements but also provides a seamless and positive user experience. And it's this commitment to quality and user satisfaction that makes our role both challenging and rewarding.

Chapter 1.2: Key Responsibilities and Challenges

Our first responsibility is defining the testing strategy. It involves outlining what needs to be tested, the testing methods to be employed, the tools required, and how the results would be reported. This strategy should align with the project's objectives and constraints and be flexible enough to adapt to changes.

Another critical responsibility is resource management. This encompasses managing the testing team, the tools, and technologies used, and the time and budget allocated for testing. As Test Managers, we oversee the recruitment and training of testers, provide them with the necessary tools and support, and ensure that the testing activities are on track and within budget.

Monitoring and controlling the testing process is also a key responsibility. We oversee the creation of test cases, the execution of tests, and the reporting of test results. We ensure that any issues identified are reported, tracked, and resolved in a timely manner.

Communication and collaboration with stakeholders are integral to our role. We work closely with project managers, developers, business analysts, and sometimes clients, ensuring everyone is aligned with the testing objectives. We regularly communicate test progress, results, and issues, enabling informed decision-making.

Along with these responsibilities come numerous challenges. One of the biggest challenges I've faced is managing change. With agile methodologies becoming the norm, requirements can change rapidly, and Test Managers need to ensure that the testing strategy and plans can accommodate these changes.

Resource constraints are another common challenge. Often, we have to manage with limited time, budget, and personnel. This requires us to be strategic in our resource allocation, prioritising tests based on risk and impact.

Keeping up with technological advancements is a constant challenge. With new testing tools and technologies emerging regularly, Test Managers need to stay updated and ensure that their teams are equipped with the right tools and skills.

Fostering a culture of quality is an ongoing challenge. As Test Managers, we need to ensure that everyone in the team understands the importance of quality and integrates quality practices into their work.

Despite these challenges, I find being a Test Manager immensely rewarding. It's a role that allows me to make a significant impact on the software product and the end-users. And every challenge overcome is an opportunity for learning and growth.

CHAPTER 2: SETTING UP

THE TESTING TEAM

The bedrock of successful test management is a competent, motivated testing team. In this chapter, we'll delve into the essentials of setting up such a team. We'll explore the criteria for selecting the right team members - individuals who not only have the necessary technical skills but also fit well within the team dynamics. We'll examine the typical team structure and the roles that team members play, understanding the unique value each role brings to the table. Lastly, we'll discuss ways to cultivate a positive team culture that fosters collaboration, continuous learning, and a shared commitment to quality. Remember, as a Test Manager, the team you assemble and how you lead them will significantly shape the success of your testing endeavours. This chapter will equip you with insights and strategies to effectively manage this responsibility.

Chapter 2.1: Selecting the Right Team Members

Assembling the right team is a critical first step in any test management journey. The performance and output of your team members will directly impact the effectiveness of your testing efforts and ultimately, the quality of the software product. Therefore, it's crucial to carefully select individuals who bring a blend of the right skills, mindset, and collaborative spirit.

When selecting team members, the primary consideration is often technical expertise. The individuals should possess a solid understanding of testing principles and methodologies. Familiarity with test automation tools, programming languages, and database management can also be significant advantages, depending on the nature of your projects.

However, technical skills alone don't guarantee a good tester. Equally important are critical thinking and problem-solving abilities. Testers need to think like the end-users and anticipate potential issues. They should be able to approach a problem from different angles, devise testing strategies, and troubleshoot issues when they arise.

Another desirable trait is attention to detail. Good testers are meticulous. They pay close attention to the smallest details, because in testing, even the minutest of oversights can lead to significant issues down the line.

Yet, the team you assemble should not consist only of individuals who share the same skills and traits. A well-rounded team should include members with diverse skills and perspectives. For example, having team members who specialise in different testing types such as functional testing, performance testing, or usability testing can greatly enhance your team's capabilities.

In addition to skills and abilities, consider how potential team members fit into the team culture. Look for individuals who are team players, open to learning and sharing their knowledge, receptive to feedback, and capable of effectively communicating their ideas and concerns. These attributes contribute to a positive, collaborative team environment.

Lastly, remember that skills can be taught, but attitude and mindset are often ingrained. Prioritise individuals who exhibit a positive, can-do attitude, a willingness to learn, and a strong work ethic. These are the individuals who will go the extra mile to ensure the quality of the product, who will continuously strive to improve their skills and processes, and who will contribute positively to the team dynamics.

In conclusion, selecting the right team members is a balance of finding individuals with the right technical skills, critical thinking abilities, and a collaborative, growth-oriented mindset. It's about putting together a diverse group of individuals who can work together towards the common goal of ensuring software quality. This careful selection process will lay a strong foundation for your testing team's success.

Chapter 2.2: Team Structure and Roles

A well-structured testing team is like a well-oiled machine, where every part plays a critical role and works seamlessly with the others to achieve the overall objective. Understanding the roles within a testing team and effectively assigning them is key to optimising your team's performance and output.

Typically, a testing team is composed of several roles, each with its own responsibilities and competencies. However, it's important to remember that these roles aren't silos; they should work in conjunction to contribute to the bigger picture. Let's delve into the core roles in a testing team.

Test Manager/Lead: The Test Manager or Lead holds the leadership role in the team. They are responsible for devising the testing strategy, managing resources, overseeing the testing process, and communicating with stakeholders. The Test Manager's primary task is to ensure that the testing objectives align with the project goals and that these objectives are met within the given constraints. Strong leadership, strategic thinking, excellent communication, and a good understanding of testing principles and methodologies are essential traits for this role.

Test Analysts: Test Analysts are the backbone of the testing team. They work closely with the Test Manager to understand the testing objectives and requirements. Their role involves creating detailed test plans, designing, and developing test cases, executing these tests, and documenting the results. Test Analysts should possess strong analytical and problem-solving skills, be detail-oriented, and have a good understanding of the software being tested.

Test Automation Engineers: In today's fast-paced software development environment, test automation has become a necessity. Test Automation Engineers are responsible for designing and implementing automated tests to speed up the testing process and increase its efficiency. This role requires a strong understanding of testing principles and a good grasp of automation tools and programming languages.

Performance Testers: Performance Testers specialise in testing the software's performance under various conditions. They conduct tests to assess aspects such as system speed, responsiveness, stability, and scalability under load. This role requires a deep understanding of performance testing principles and tools, and often, knowledge of network and system architecture.

Security Testers: With cybersecurity becoming a major concern, Security Testers play a crucial role in the team. They conduct tests to identify potential security vulnerabilities in the software and suggest measures to mitigate these risks. This role demands a solid understanding of information security principles and testing methodologies.

Usability Testers: Usability Testers focus on the user's perspective. They conduct tests to assess the software's usability, ensuring it's user-friendly, intuitive, and meets the users' needs. Strong empathy, good understanding of usability principles, and often, knowledge of user experience design, are important for this role.

A well-structured testing team should ideally encompass all these roles. However, the size and composition of your team will depend on various factors such as the nature and scope of the project, the project's constraints, and the organisation's testing philosophy. Sometimes, team members may need to wear multiple hats and take up more than one role. Regardless of the team structure you adopt, remember that communication and collaboration are key. Each role, while distinct, should be geared towards the common goal of delivering a high-quality software product. This collaborative approach will optimise your team's performance, enhance the software's quality, and contribute to a successful project outcome.

Chapter 2.3: Fostering a Positive Team Culture

In my years of managing testing teams, I have come to appreciate the profound impact team culture has on performance, productivity, and overall job satisfaction. A positive team culture fosters collaboration, boosts morale, and motivates team members to strive for excellence. Conversely, a negative culture can hinder communication, create conflicts, and lower team members' motivation and engagement. Therefore, as Test Managers, one of our key responsibilities is to cultivate a positive team culture.

One of the pillars of a positive team culture is open and transparent communication. It's important to encourage team members to freely share their ideas, concerns, and feedback. Regular team meetings, one-on-one catchups, and open-door policies can facilitate this. Also, make sure that important information, such as project updates, changes, and decisions, is promptly and clearly communicated to all team members. This not only keeps everyone on the same page but also builds trust and respect.

Another key aspect of a positive team culture is collaboration. Team members should feel that they are part of a team, working together towards a common goal. Promote a collaborative environment where team members support each other, share their knowledge and experiences, and jointly solve problems. This can be encouraged through team building activities, pair testing sessions, or joint problem-solving exercises. Remember, the whole is often greater than the sum of its parts, and a collaborative team is much more effective than individuals working in silos.

Recognition and appreciation play a significant role in fostering a positive team culture. Regularly acknowledge and celebrate team members' achievements, big or small. This can be as simple as a verbal appreciation in a team meeting or a formal recognition in the company's communication channels. Recognition not only boosts the individuals' morale but also motivates others in the team to strive for excellence.

Learning and development opportunities are another crucial element of a positive team culture. Encourage team members to continuously upgrade their skills and knowledge. This could be through training sessions, workshops, conferences, or online courses. Also, promote a culture of learning from mistakes. Instead of penalising errors, use them as learning opportunities, helping team members understand what went wrong and how it can be avoided in the future. This approach fosters a growth mindset and shows team members that you value their growth and development.

Foster a culture of quality. Make quality a priority in all your team's activities and decisions. Instil in your team members the belief that everyone is responsible for the software's quality, not just the testers. Encourage them to consider quality at every stage of the development process, from requirement gathering and design to coding and deployment. This culture of quality not only enhances the product's quality but also gives team members a sense of pride and satisfaction in their work.

In conclusion, fostering a positive team culture is a continuous effort. It's about creating an environment where team members feel valued, supported, and motivated to do their best. And while it takes time and effort, the benefits - enhanced team performance, high-quality deliverables, and a satisfied, motivated team - make it well worth the investment.

CHAPTER 3: PLANNING AND STRATEGY

Solid planning and a robust strategy form the backbone of effective software testing. In this chapter, we will delve into the elements that define the testing direction and outline the steps required to meet our goals. Firstly, we'll examine how to develop a comprehensive test strategy that aligns with your project's goals and constraints. Next, we'll walk you through the process of creating an effective test plan, a blueprint that details the who, what, when, and how of the testing process. Lastly, we'll explore risk-based testing planning, an approach that prioritises testing efforts based on the potential risks associated with the software's features. The methodologies and techniques we will discuss here are crucial for every Test Manager to master, enabling you to direct your testing efforts effectively and maximise your resources.

Chapter 3.1: Developing a Test Strategy

Developing a test strategy is an indispensable step in the testing process. It provides a roadmap for your testing efforts, defining the overall approach and guiding your team to achieve the testing objectives effectively and efficiently. A well-crafted test strategy can significantly enhance your testing efforts' effectiveness, while a poorly defined strategy can lead to wastage of resources and jeopardise the software's quality.

When developing a test strategy, the first step is to understand the project's objectives and constraints. What are the software's intended functionality and performance? What are the timeframes and resources available for testing? What are the risks associated with the software and its features? The answers to these questions will help you define your testing goals and determine your approach.

Next, define the scope of your testing efforts. Identify the features and functionalities that will be tested and those that won't. This is crucial to ensure that your team's efforts are focused on the right areas and that critical features aren't overlooked.

Once the scope is defined, decide on the testing levels and types to be employed. Will you conduct unit testing, integration testing, system testing, or acceptance testing? Will you perform functional testing, performance testing, security testing, or usability testing? The choice will depend on the nature of the software, the project's constraints, and the identified risks.

An essential part of your test strategy is determining the testing techniques and tools. Will you use manual or automated testing, or a combination of both? What testing methodologies will you follow - black box, white box, or grey box? What testing tools will you use? The choices should align with your testing goals and the team's expertise.

Additionally, define the test environment requirements. What hardware, software, and network conditions are needed to simulate the end-user environment? Ensuring a suitable test environment is critical to obtaining accurate and reliable test results.

Your test strategy should also outline the test data requirements. Test data plays a crucial role in testing, and you should define what data is needed, how it will be obtained or created, and how it will be managed and protected.

Lastly, determine the criteria for starting and stopping the tests, and define what constitutes a successful test. These criteria provide a clear direction for your team and help avoid confusion and conflicts.

Once your test strategy is developed, communicate it to all relevant stakeholders. This not only ensures everyone is on the same page but also gives them an opportunity to provide their inputs, which can further enhance your strategy.

In conclusion, developing a test strategy is a thoughtful and meticulous process. It requires a deep understanding of the software, the project's objectives and constraints, and the principles and methodologies of testing. A well-defined test strategy will guide your team's efforts, optimise the use of resources, and significantly enhance the software's quality. Therefore, as Test Managers, it is an area that we must master and continually refine.

Chapter 3.2: Creating an Effective Test Plan

The Test Plan, a detailed guide for the testing process, is a crucial artifact in any software testing cycle. It provides a clear roadmap of what needs to be tested, how it will be tested, who will do the testing, and when it will be done. An effective Test Plan enables systematic testing, ensures optimal utilisation of resources, and helps to maintain a consistent and coordinated approach across the team.

The first step in creating an effective Test Plan is understanding the software's requirements and objectives. Carefully analyse the project documentation, engage in discussions with the project stakeholders, and try to grasp the product's intended functionality, performance, and other essential characteristics. This understanding is the foundation upon which the rest of your Test Plan will be built.

Next, define the scope of testing. This includes identifying the features to be tested and specifying those that are out of scope. Prioritise the functionalities based on their criticality, complexity, and risk. A well-defined scope ensures that the team's efforts are focused on the right areas, maximising the effectiveness of the testing process.

Once the scope is defined, outline the testing approach and techniques. Describe the testing levels (unit, integration, system, etc.) and types (functional, performance, usability, etc.) that will be carried out. Specify whether manual or automated testing will be used, or a combination of both. Also, identify the testing tools that will be used.

Your Test Plan should also specify the test environment setup, detailing the hardware, software, and network conditions needed for testing. This is crucial because the test environment should ideally mirror the end-user environment to achieve reliable and valid test results.

Another critical component of the Test Plan is the test schedule. Define when each testing activity will begin and end, and allocate time for bug fixing and retesting. Make sure to factor in buffer time for unexpected delays. The schedule should align with the overall project timeline and be realistic, considering the team's capabilities and the resources available.

The Test Plan must also define the roles and responsibilities. Identify who will perform the testing, who will manage the testing process, who will handle bug fixes, and so on. Clearly defined roles and responsibilities help avoid confusion and ensure accountability.

An effective Test Plan also outlines the procedure for bug tracking and reporting. Specify the tools that will be used for bug tracking, the process for reporting bugs, and the protocol for communicating bugs to the development team.

Your Test Plan should also specify the exit criteria - conditions under which testing will be considered complete. These can include factors such as the percentage of test cases passed, the severity of unresolved bugs, the completion of regression testing, and so on.

Lastly, the Test Plan should describe the process for test review and revision. This includes how and when the tests will be reviewed, who will perform the review, and the process for updating the tests based on feedback.

Remember, the Test Plan is a dynamic document. It should be regularly updated to reflect changes in project requirements, scope, timeline, or resources.

In conclusion, creating an effective Test Plan is a meticulous process that requires a deep understanding of the software, its requirements, the project's constraints, and the testing principles and methodologies. A well-crafted Test Plan not only guides your team's efforts and facilitates communication among stakeholders but also contributes significantly to the success of the testing process and the quality of the final product. As Test Managers, we must excel in this crucial skill.

Chapter 3.3: Risk-Based Testing Planning

Risk-based testing planning is an approach that allows us to focus our testing efforts based on the potential risks or defects that could critically impact the software's functionality or performance. This strategy is instrumental in optimising resources, prioritising testing activities, and enhancing the effectiveness of the testing process.

The initial step in risk-based testing planning is risk identification. Start by understanding the software and its intended use and identify potential areas where defects could occur. Risks could stem from complex functionality, new or untested technology, significant changes in requirements, or integration with other software, to name a few. This process may require collaboration with different stakeholders, including developers, business analysts, and users, to gain a comprehensive understanding of potential risks.

Once the risks are identified, the next step is risk analysis, where each risk is evaluated based on its potential impact and the probability of occurrence. Impact refers to the severity of the defect on the software or the end user, while the probability of occurrence is the likelihood of the defect happening. Each risk can be categorised as high, medium, or low, based on this analysis. This assessment helps in prioritising the risks, and consequently, the testing activities.

Following the risk analysis, the third step is risk mitigation. For each identified risk, define a strategy to reduce the likelihood of occurrence or minimise the impact. These strategies could include specific testing techniques, more rigorous testing of certain functionalities, or involving more experienced testers. In some cases, risk mitigation might also involve discussions with the development team for potential design changes to reduce the risk.

After the mitigation strategies are defined, you can formulate your test plan based on the risk priorities. High-risk areas should be tested first and perhaps more thoroughly than areas with less associated risk. This approach not only ensures that the most critical areas are tested early but also helps in optimal allocation of resources. Remember, the goal is not to eliminate all risk but to manage it effectively.

Risk-based testing planning also requires regular monitoring and review. Risks should be reassessed throughout the project life cycle, as changes in requirements, design, or other factors could affect the risk profile. Any changes should be communicated to all stakeholders and the test plan should be adjusted accordingly.

In conclusion, risk-based testing planning is a strategic approach that guides your testing efforts based on potential risks. It requires a good understanding of the software, its usage, and the project's constraints, as well as the ability to analyse and prioritise risks effectively. This approach not only enhances the effectiveness of your testing process but also contributes significantly to the software's quality. As Test Managers, mastering risk-based testing planning is a critical skill that can greatly enhance our ability to deliver high-quality software in a resource-effective manner.

CHAPTER 4: TEST ESTIMATION AND BUDGETING

In the realm of software testing, success isn't solely measured by the identification and resolution of defects; it also includes the prudent use of resources. Efficiently managing the allocation of time and budget is a cornerstone of effective test management. Hence, in this chapter, we explore the vital aspects of test estimation and budgeting, presenting practical techniques and strategies that can help streamline these processes.

One of the most challenging aspects of test management is providing accurate test estimates. The process of estimating the resources, effort, and time required for testing is crucial for test planning and scheduling. This estimation feeds into the broader project planning and has significant implications for the project's timeline and budget. Our first focus, 'Techniques for Test Estimation', delves into popular methods such as Function Point Analysis, Use Case Point Method, and Test Point Analysis. We'll also cover approaches that lean on historical data and heuristic methods.

Estimation directly feeds into the second part of this chapter, 'Allocating and Managing Test Budgets'. The allocated budget is a vital constraint that influences the test strategy, scope, schedule, and resources. We'll look at how to allocate the test budget effectively, considering factors such as project scope, risk, quality requirements, and resources. Furthermore, we'll delve into managing this budget throughout the project lifecycle, addressing potential overruns and re-allocating funds in light of changing requirements or unforeseen challenges.

Chapter 4 thus serves as a guide to navigate the tricky terrain of test estimation and budgeting. The principles and practices covered in this chapter will arm you with the necessary skills to make informed decisions and efficiently utilise resources, contributing significantly to the project's overall success.

Chapter 4.1: Techniques for Test Estimation

Test estimation is a crucial process in test management, determining the time, effort, and resources required to test a software product effectively. It directly influences the testing schedule and the project's overall timeline and budget. Several techniques can help us perform test estimation more accurately. Here, we delve into some of the most commonly used methods.

Function Point Analysis (FPA) is a widely used technique that assesses the functionality provided by the software. It measures the software's size based on the user's point of view, considering inputs, outputs, inquiries, interfaces, and data tables. By relating past data of how long it took to test function points, we can estimate the required testing effort.

The Use Case Point Method is another technique based on the software's functionality. Here, we estimate the testing effort based on use cases - the interactions between the software and its users.

Each use case is assigned a complexity level (simple, average, or complex), and the sum gives us the Use Case Points (UCP). As with FPA, past data can be used to determine the testing effort per UCP.

The Test Point Analysis (TPA) method focuses on the test process itself. It uses factors such as the number of test cases, test levels, and test complexity to estimate the testing effort. The TPA approach is particularly useful for projects with detailed test specifications.

While these structured approaches offer valuable frameworks, heuristic methods, like expert judgment and analogous estimation, are beneficial when historical data is sparse, or the project scope is poorly defined. Expert judgment involves using the experience and knowledge of testing experts to predict the testing effort, while analogous estimation compares the current project with similar past projects to forecast the effort needed.

Experience-based techniques like Work Breakdown Structure (WBS) can also be instrumental. Here, we break down the testing project into smaller, manageable tasks. Estimating the effort for each task often yields a more accurate overall estimate, as it is easier to foresee the effort needed for smaller activities.

An approach that considers risk is Risk-Based Estimation. It focuses on potential risks associated with the software and prioritises testing efforts towards the functionalities with higher risks. This technique often leads to more efficient resource allocation and a higher return on investment.

Lastly, another method is the Three-Point Estimation technique, borrowed from project management practices. It calculates the most likely estimate based on the best-case, most likely, and worst-case scenarios, considering uncertainties and risks.

In conclusion, test estimation is a multifaceted process with no one-size-fits-all solution. Different projects may require different methods, or even a combination of techniques, to achieve an accurate estimate. It requires a good understanding of the software, its requirements, the project's constraints, and the testing principles and methodologies. Historical data, if available, can be a valuable input. Accurate test estimation not only helps in effective test planning but also facilitates communication with other stakeholders and contributes significantly to the project's overall management and success. As Test Managers, mastering test estimation techniques is an indispensable skill that enhances our ability to manage testing activities efficiently.

Chapter 4.2: Allocating and Managing Test Budgets

Budgeting is a critical aspect of test management. The allocation and management of financial resources can have a profound impact on the quality of the testing process and, consequently, the quality of the final software product.

At the beginning of a project, a test manager is tasked with defining the test budget. This budget is usually a subset of the overall project budget and must be used to cover all costs related to testing activities. These might include personnel salaries, hardware and software resources, training, and any additional costs related to third-party services or specialised tools.

The process of allocating the test budget should be based on a thorough understanding of the testing requirements and the resources required to fulfil them. This understanding is largely derived from the test estimation process we discussed in the previous section. Historical data from past projects can provide valuable insights into average costs and potential pitfalls, while the project's risk profile can guide the allocation of funds towards riskier areas of the software.

One crucial aspect of budget allocation is ensuring that sufficient funds are allocated to every phase of the testing lifecycle. For instance, it can be tempting to focus heavily on the execution phase, but this can result in underfunding of essential activities like test planning, designing, and review. An imbalance in allocation can lead to issues down the line, including rushed planning, overlooked defects, and inadequate reporting.

From my early days as a Test Manager. We were working on a project with a tight budget, and in an effort to maximise resources, we decided to skimp on the budget for test planning and design. We believed that our experienced team could manage with less rigorous planning. Unfortunately, this decision came back to bite us during the execution phase. Many unexpected scenarios arose that we hadn't adequately prepared for. We ended up spending significantly more time and resources on debugging and retesting than we would have if we had invested more in the planning phase. This experience taught me the importance of balanced budget allocation across all phases of testing.

Once the budget is allocated, managing it effectively is crucial. This involves monitoring expenditures, identifying, and addressing any deviations, and re-allocating funds, as necessary. Good budget management also involves being prepared for unforeseen expenses and challenges. Changes in project scope, unexpected defects, and modifications in project timelines can all impact the test budget.

An essential aspect of managing the test budget is regular communication with the project stakeholders. Keeping them informed about the status of the budget and any potential issues can help prevent surprises and enable more informed decision-making. Transparent reporting on the allocation and usage of the budget can also help demonstrate the value provided by the testing team and justify the investment in testing activities.

In conclusion, the effective allocation and management of the test budget is a critical responsibility of the Test Manager. By understanding the testing requirements, using accurate test estimations, and managing and communicating the budget effectively, Test Managers can ensure the efficient use of resources, avoid cost overruns, and contribute to the overall success of the project.

CHAPTER 5: TEST DESIGN

AND DEVELOPMENT

Following the intricacies of planning, estimation, and budgeting, we now approach the pivotal phase of Test Design and Development. This critical stage of the testing lifecycle involves translating our meticulously laid out plans into tangible actions that will guide the actual testing process. This chapter unravels key areas such as overseeing test case design, test data management, and managing test environment setup.

The first subtopic, "Overseeing Test Case Design", delves into the creation of effective test cases - a vital component of any testing initiative. Test cases form the basis for executing tests, providing detailed steps to verify the software's functionality and its alignment with user requirements. This segment will explore practical tips for designing robust, comprehensive test cases. We will consider factors such as the complexity of the application under test, business requirements, potential risks, and the targeted user experience. The creation of test cases isn't a solitary task; it requires collaboration with business analysts, developers, and sometimes even the end-users, ensuring the end product delivers what it promises.

Our next focus is "Test Data Management". An often-underestimated aspect of software testing, test data plays a critical role in the overall efficacy of our testing efforts. Quality test data contributes significantly to robust testing, as it helps mimic real-world scenarios and user interactions. We'll explore strategies for identifying, creating, and managing test data, maintaining data integrity, and ensuring privacy, especially when dealing with sensitive user information.

Finally, we'll venture into "Managing Test Environment Setup". A well-configured test environment mirrors the product's live environment, enabling testers to identify potential issues before deployment. However, setting up and maintaining such an environment can pose numerous challenges. We'll cover techniques for managing different environments, ensuring consistency across them, and troubleshooting common problems.

The concept of designing and developing tests is akin to turning a blueprint into a fully functional building. It requires meticulous attention to detail, a firm grasp of the system's functionalities, and a deep understanding of the end-users' needs and expectations. Just as an architect supervises the transformation of their design into a structure, as test managers, we oversee the conversion of our test strategy and plans into tangible test cases, ensuring the software product aligns with its expected outcomes.

Beyond the technical aspects, this phase also requires a delicate balancing act. We're often caught in the crosshairs of competing constraints – time, resources, and the ever-present demand for high-quality software. Striking the right balance becomes a testament to a test manager's skills, experience, and judgment.

This chapter thus presents an in-depth understanding of test design and development, emphasising the interplay between various components and highlighting the importance of a comprehensive approach. It aims to equip you with practical knowledge, whether you're designing test cases for a complex, multi-layered system, managing large volumes of test data, or setting up a test environment that accurately mimics the live setting.

A nuanced understanding of these elements will empower you to design tests that are both effective and efficient, thereby enhancing the quality of the software and ensuring a better end-user experience. It's not just about finding bugs; it's about paving the way to software that performs impeccably in the real world, software that meets and exceeds user expectations. In the end, successful test design and development significantly contribute to the triumphant realisation of this goal.

Chapter 5.1: Overseeing Test Case Design

Test case design serves as the backbone of the testing process, converting the test strategy and plan into a step-by-step guide for executing tests. The creation of a well-structured, comprehensive test case can make the difference between a thoroughly vetted software product and one that slips through the cracks, harbouring undiscovered defects.

One of the first steps in designing test cases is identifying and understanding the software requirements. These can be derived from various sources, including requirement documents, user stories, use cases, and discussions with stakeholders. The requirements should be scrutinised for clarity, completeness, and testability. Ambiguities and gaps should be addressed at this stage to prevent potential misunderstandings that could lead to flawed test cases.

Once the requirements are clear, the design process can begin. Each test case should aim to verify a specific requirement or part of a requirement. The test case should outline the steps to be followed, the data to be entered, the expected outcome, and the criteria for determining whether the test has passed or failed.

Here, it's vital to keep in mind the principle of traceability - every test case should be traceable back to a requirement. This ensures coverage of all requirements and makes it easier to identify which part of the software is affected when a test case fails.

It's also crucial to consider the different possible scenarios, including edge cases and negative scenarios. For instance, a requirement might specify that a user can enter a valid email address. A test case to verify this requirement would not only test the functionality with a valid email address but also attempt to enter an invalid address to ensure the software behaves as expected in this scenario.

As the test cases are developed, they should be reviewed regularly. Reviewing could involve other testers, business analysts, developers, or other stakeholders. Regular reviews help identify gaps, inconsistencies, and redundancies early on and improve the overall quality of the test cases.

In addition, it's crucial to maintain a dynamic approach to test case design. Software development is often an iterative process, and as changes are made to the software, corresponding changes will likely be required in the test cases. Keeping the test cases up to date ensures they remain relevant and effective throughout the project.

Overseeing test case design also involves considering the maintainability and reusability of the test cases. Test cases that are well-organised, clearly written, and modular can be more easily updated and reused in future projects, reducing the effort required for test case design in the long term.

An often overlooked but essential part of test case design is the documentation. Good documentation ensures that the information about the test case, its purpose, its creation and modification history, and its relationship to other test cases and requirements is preserved. This not only aids in understanding and executing the test case but also helps in troubleshooting issues, performing impact analysis, and training new team members.

In conclusion, overseeing test case design involves much more than simply ensuring the creation of test cases. It requires a deep understanding of the software and its requirements, a strategic approach to verify all aspects of the software, and a focus on maintainability and reusability. It also requires effective collaboration and communication within the team and with other stakeholders. The design of robust, comprehensive test cases significantly contributes to the identification of defects, the enhancement of software quality, and the success of the software product in meeting user expectations.

Chapter 5.2: Test Data Management

Test data management is a fundamental yet frequently underestimated aspect of software testing. The quality and relevance of test data can significantly influence the effectiveness and efficiency of your testing efforts. Furthermore, in a world where data is both a critical resource and a potential liability, managing test data appropriately is paramount.

Test data are the inputs that you provide to the software to perform testing. To ensure realistic and comprehensive testing, this data should closely mimic the variety, complexity, and volume of data that the software will handle in the real world.

Designing and creating appropriate test data involves understanding the software's functionality, the different types of data it will handle, and the various scenarios in which it will be used. This includes understanding the expected use cases, as well as the edge cases that may push the software to its limits.

For example, if you are testing a banking software that processes transactions, you would need test data that represents different types of transactions (withdrawals, deposits, transfers, etc.), various amounts (from small transactions to very large ones), and different scenarios (normal processing, insufficient funds, fraudulent transactions, etc.).

Managing test data also involves maintaining data integrity. If the software involves complex transactions or workflows that span multiple test cases, you need to ensure that the state of the data is maintained correctly throughout these test cases. This could involve creating a separate dataset for each test case or ensuring that the test cases are executed in a particular sequence.

In the age of big data and machine learning, test data management can also involve handling large volumes of data. If the software you are testing needs to handle big data, you would need to generate or acquire test data in sufficient volume to replicate these conditions.

One of the key challenges in test data management is maintaining privacy and compliance, especially when dealing with sensitive data such as personal identifiable information (PII) or financial data. If you are using real data for testing, you need to ensure that this data is anonymised or de-identified to protect privacy and comply with data protection regulations.

This can involve techniques such as data masking, where sensitive data elements are replaced with fictitious yet realistic data, or synthetic data generation, where entirely artificial data is generated that mimics the properties and patterns of real data.

Managing test data involves the storage, retrieval, and maintenance of the data. This includes storing the data securely, organising it in a way that it can be easily accessed and used for testing, and maintaining it to ensure it remains relevant and accurate as the software and its requirements evolve.

In conclusion, test data management is an integral part of the testing process. Effective test data management enables realistic and comprehensive testing, aids in the identification of defects, and ensures compliance with privacy and data protection standards. As a test manager, being well-versed in the principles and techniques of test data management will equip you to handle the data-related challenges of testing and enhance the overall quality of your testing efforts.

Chapter 5.3: Managing Test Environment Setup

A well-structured test environment closely simulates the live setting, allowing for effective replication of user scenarios and thorough testing of software performance. However, setting up and managing such an environment introduces its own complexities. These complexities encompass aspects like hardware configuration, software setup, network settings, and database management, among others.

A testing environment consists of hardware, software, and network configurations that support the test executions. It should mirror the production environment as closely as possible to unveil potential issues before the software's actual deployment. The closer the test environment is to the production setting, the higher the chance of detecting bugs that might occur in the live environment.

Choosing the right hardware and software is crucial. You need to ensure that your test environment has similar servers, operating systems, databases, and browsers to the production environment. Understanding these needs is crucial to enable a holistic replication of the user's interaction with the application. For instance, if the software is expected to run on multiple browser types and versions, your test environment should cater to these variations.

Network settings form a key part of this setup. Configuring the network in the test environment to resemble the production environment is crucial for performance testing. Elements such as bandwidth, latency, and security settings should be carefully planned and implemented. A miscalculation here might lead to performance glitches being missed during the testing phase, only to surface later when the application goes live.

When setting up databases for your test environment, it's vital to ensure they mirror the production databases. Size, structure, data distribution – all these aspects should be as close to the live scenario as possible. Test data should be carefully managed, ensuring that it covers all possible variations that may occur in production.

Another crucial aspect of test environment management is monitoring and maintenance. Regular checks and balances are required to ensure the continued integrity of the test environment. Over time, changes in the software or hardware, updates, or anomalies may cause the test environment to drift from its initial setup. Regular maintenance helps in early detection and resolution of these discrepancies.

Moreover, as a test manager, managing the access and usage of the test environment is a responsibility that you bear. Ensuring that changes and updates to the environment are controlled and documented can prevent unforeseen issues and help in troubleshooting when problems arise.

One must not forget the need for multiple test environments, such as development, quality assurance, and staging environments. Each serves a unique purpose and requires careful management. Keeping them isolated from each other prevents cross-contamination and enables controlled testing. Yet, they should be kept as consistent as possible to ensure that a software release passes through the same conditions in each environment.

Furthermore, modern cloud-based environments offer new opportunities and challenges for test environment management. They offer greater flexibility, scalability, and cost-effectiveness, but also require knowledge of cloud management and security practices.

In essence, managing a test environment setup isn't just a one-time task, but a continuous process that requires vigilance, technical acumen, and solid management skills. It involves careful planning, consistent monitoring, and regular updates. As a test manager, you will find that investing time and effort in managing the test environment setup can significantly enhance the efficiency and effectiveness of your testing efforts, thereby contributing to the development of a high-quality software product.

CHAPTER 6: TEST EXECUTION AND MONITORING

The essence of software testing lies in test execution and monitoring - the phase where all the plans and preparations culminate into actionable tasks. This pivotal stage holds the key to the discovery of software flaws, gaps in requirements, and sometimes, unexpected areas of improvement. As a test manager, you oversee this process, ensuring not only that testing proceeds according to plan but also that problems are addressed promptly, progress is monitored, and stakeholders are kept informed.

Test execution involves the running of test cases that have been meticulously designed and developed in the preceding stages. However, it is not a mere process of running tests and recording the results. As a test manager, it requires strategic allocation of resources, deciding the sequence of test execution based on test dependencies and risks, and managing the test execution schedule.

Tracking the progress of test execution forms an integral part of this stage. This task requires a focus on the granularity of test cases, understanding which functionalities have been tested, which ones are left, and how many have passed or failed. This tracking provides invaluable insights into the status of the testing process and can help identify potential bottlenecks or areas that need further attention. Various test management tools can assist with this task, providing visual and quantitative aids to comprehend the process's progress better.

An inevitable aspect of test execution is encountering issues. Test execution issues can stem from a variety of sources - bugs in the software, discrepancies in test data, shortcomings in the test environment, or even unanticipated software behaviour. As the test manager, it is your role to swiftly identify these issues, comprehend their implications, and devise an effective resolution strategy. This could involve liaising with the development team for bug fixes, adjusting test data or environment configurations, or updating the test cases to align with the software's actual behaviour.

A significant part of test monitoring is reporting the test status. Transparency with stakeholders about the testing process's progress is vital for overall project management and for maintaining trust within the team. This includes conveying information about completed tests, discovered defects, resolved and unresolved issues, and the impact on the project timeline and objectives. The frequency and detail of these reports may vary depending on the stakeholders' requirements, but the underlying principle remains the same - keeping the stakeholders informed about the testing progress.

In this chapter, we will delve deeper into these aspects of test execution and monitoring. We will explore how to effectively track test progress, devise strategies for handling test execution issues, and best practices for reporting test status to stakeholders. As we navigate through these topics, remember that test execution and monitoring are dynamic processes. They require adaptability and continuous learning, leveraging every encountered issue as an opportunity to refine your testing process and contribute to the software's quality.

As we embark on this journey, it is crucial to remember that while the primary objective is to identify software defects, the ultimate goal is to ensure the delivery of a product that aligns with user expectations and business objectives. So, let's take a step forward in unravelling the intricacies of test execution and monitoring - the stage where testing transitions from planning to action.

Chapter 6.1: Tracking Test Progress

Tracking test progress is a crucial responsibility of a test manager during the test execution phase. This process, conducted meticulously, provides insights into the project's current status, facilitates timely decision-making, and ensures effective resource allocation. Furthermore, it enables early identification and resolution of potential bottlenecks that could impact the overall project timeline and quality.

The foundation of tracking test progress lies in clearly defined metrics and Key Performance Indicators (KPIs). These could include the number of executed test cases, passed and failed tests, discovered defects, resolved issues, and their severity. These metrics, while providing a quantitative measure of progress, must be complemented with qualitative insights like the reasons for test failures, the areas of the software that are more prone to defects, and potential risks in the remaining test schedule.

Tracking test progress also requires a well-structured approach to managing test documentation. This includes maintaining up-to-date records of test plans, test cases, and test results. Tools like spreadsheets or specialised test management software can be employed to keep track of these documents, provide an overview of test progress, and highlight areas needing attention.

A crucial aspect of tracking test progress is understanding dependencies between different parts of the software and their corresponding test cases. This involves determining which tests can be executed in parallel, which ones must be run in sequence, and how defects in one area of the software might affect other areas. This understanding enables prioritisation of test activities, effective management of the test schedule, and accurate prediction of the testing process's trajectory.

Another critical facet of tracking test progress is monitoring the resolution of discovered defects. This involves working closely with the development team to ensure defects are fixed promptly, retesting the fixed areas, and validating that the fixes haven't introduced new issues. This feedback loop between testing and development is a key driver of the software quality improvement process.

In the ever-evolving landscape of software development methodologies, tracking test progress must adapt to fit different approaches. In traditional waterfall models, test progress tracking might focus on the completion of distinct testing stages. In contrast, Agile or DevOps approaches would require tracking progress within each sprint or iteration, with a greater emphasis on continuous integration and continuous testing.

Ultimately, tracking test progress is a dynamic, ongoing process that demands attention to detail, communication, and flexibility. By tracking progress effectively, you not only ensure that the testing process stays on track but also contribute to enhancing the software's quality, maintaining project schedules, and ensuring efficient utilisation of resources. Through this process, you pave the way for delivering a software product that meets the expectations of stakeholders and end users.

Chapter 6.2: Handling Test Execution Issues

Test execution is where the rubber meets the road in the software testing process. During this phase, test cases come to life as testers delve into the software's functionalities, stress-testing them against various inputs, conditions, and scenarios. While this phase can be quite revealing, it is not without its share of challenges. As a test manager, one of your critical responsibilities is to effectively handle these test execution issues, ensuring they don't impede the progress of the testing process.

Test execution issues come in various forms, from unexpected software behaviours and defects to shortcomings in the test environment or discrepancies in test data. Each issue presents its own set of challenges and requires a unique resolution strategy. Understanding the nature of the issue is the first step towards its resolution.

When a test case fails, the first thing to ascertain is whether the failure is due to a defect in the software or an issue with the test case itself. It involves carefully reviewing the failed test case, the associated requirements, and the actual software behaviour. If the failure is due to a software defect, it needs to be promptly reported to the development team with all necessary details to reproduce and resolve the issue.

Sometimes, test execution issues stem from discrepancies in test data or configuration issues in the test environment. These issues might lead to failed test cases, even if the software is functioning correctly. In such cases, the resolution strategy would involve identifying and rectifying the discrepancy in test data or resolving the configuration issue in the test environment.

Test execution issues may also arise from unexpected software behaviour that isn't necessarily a defect but wasn't anticipated when designing the test cases. Such issues pose unique challenges, requiring a revaluation of the test case design or even the software requirements.

Handling test execution issues isn't just about resolving the issues themselves but also about managing their impact on the test execution schedule. Delays in resolving issues can lead to delays in test execution, potentially impacting the overall project timeline. Therefore, it's vital to maintain open lines of communication with the development team, ensuring that issues are resolved promptly, and testing can proceed according to schedule.

Effective handling of test execution issues also involves keeping the stakeholders informed. Regularly updating stakeholders about the status of test execution, encountered issues, and their resolution status fosters transparency and maintains trust. It also helps manage expectations regarding the testing process's progress and the potential impact on project timelines.

Furthermore, handling test execution issues offers valuable learning opportunities. Each encountered issue is a chance to improve the testing process, be it by refining test case design, enhancing the test environment setup, or improving test data management.

Leveraging these learning opportunities leads to continuous improvement, contributing to the delivery of high-quality software.

Managing test execution issues is a critical aspect of the test manager's role, requiring problem-solving skills, effective communication, and adaptability. While these issues pose challenges, they also open doors for improvement and refinement of the testing process. By effectively handling these issues, you ensure the smooth progress of the test execution phase, contributing to the delivery of a software product that meets the expectations of the users and stakeholders.

Chapter 6.3: Reporting Test Status to Stakeholders

Reporting the status of tests is not simply a task to complete but a fundamental part of the strategic communication process within a project. It holds significant importance in maintaining transparency with stakeholders about the progress of the testing process, the encountered issues, and their implications on the project timeline and objectives. As a test manager, this responsibility falls primarily on your shoulders, requiring you to provide accurate, timely, and comprehensive updates to stakeholders.

Creating an effective test status report begins with understanding the audience, their information needs, and their role in the project. Different stakeholders may require different levels of detail. For instance, while a project manager might need a detailed breakdown of test progress, defect status, and potential risks, an executive might prefer a high-level summary of the overall test status and its impact on project milestones.

The next step is to decide on the content and format of the report. The content should cover key test metrics such as the number of executed, passed, and failed test cases, discovered defects and their severity, and the status of issue resolution. It should also include a section on the test execution schedule, outlining completed stages, ongoing activities, and upcoming tasks.

While numerical metrics provide quantitative insights into test progress, they should be supplemented with a qualitative analysis. This could include an explanation of encountered issues, their impact on the test progress, and the actions taken to resolve them. It could also cover areas of the software that are more prone to defects, potential risks in the upcoming test activities, and recommendations for improvement.

The format of the report should be clear, concise, and easy to understand. Visual aids like charts, graphs, or tables can be extremely useful in conveying complex information in a digestible manner. A well-structured report often starts with a summary, followed by detailed sections on various aspects of the test status, and ends with a conclusion highlighting the key takeaways.

The frequency of reporting the test status depends on the stakeholders' needs and the project context. In some cases, a weekly update might be sufficient, while in others, daily updates may be required. Timely reporting is crucial to ensure that stakeholders stay informed about the testing process's progress and can make informed decisions.

Reporting test status is not just about providing information but also about managing expectations. It's essential to be honest and transparent about the test progress, even if it involves delivering unwelcome news. It's always better to share problems as they arise, rather than surprising stakeholders with unexpected delays or quality issues later on.

While the task of reporting test status can seem daunting, remember that it's an integral part of your role as a test manager. It ensures effective communication with stakeholders, contributes to overall project management, and fosters a culture of transparency and accountability. By keeping stakeholders informed about the test status, you not only uphold the integrity of the testing process but also contribute to the successful delivery of a high-quality software product that meets the expectations of users and stakeholders.

CHAPTER 7: ISSUE

MANAGEMENT

In the dynamic realm of software testing, issue management stands as a significant pillar of the test manager's responsibilities. This multifaceted function is crucial for maintaining the quality of the software product, adhering to the project timelines, and ensuring efficient resource utilisation. A smooth and well-organised issue management process helps in mitigating potential risks and maintains the software's integrity. This chapter focuses on the intricacies of issue management, guiding you through its key stages - identification, resolution, and communication.

To begin, we delve into 'Identifying and Classifying Issues' in Chapter 7.1. As test managers, we will encounter a diverse range of issues, from defects in the software to problems in the test environment, discrepancies in test data, or challenges in the test execution process. Recognising these issues at the earliest stage is the first crucial step towards addressing them. This is closely followed by classifying these issues based on their nature, impact, severity, and priority. This classification plays a vital role in determining the resolution strategy and prioritising issue handling.

Chapter 7.2, 'Managing Issue Resolution', focuses on the next stage of issue management. Having identified and classified the issues, the focus shifts to resolving these issues effectively and promptly. This could involve liaising with the development team for defect fixes, tweaking the test environment setup, or revising the test data. This chapter delves into strategies for managing issue resolution, including prioritising issues, coordinating with different teams, and ensuring the timely resolution of issues.

Finally, in Chapter 7.3, 'Reporting and Communicating about Issues', we discuss the critical role of communication in issue management. Keeping stakeholders informed about the status of issues and their resolution progress fosters transparency and maintains trust. This involves not only reporting the current status but also managing expectations about potential delays or quality issues that may arise due to these issues. We will explore the strategies for effective communication and reporting about issues, including deciding on the content, format, and frequency of the reports, understanding the information needs of different stakeholders, and ensuring honest and timely communication.

Issue management is a challenging yet rewarding aspect of the test manager's role. It requires a blend of problem-solving skills, technical expertise, communication skills, and adaptability. As we journey through this chapter, we aim to equip you with the knowledge and skills to manage issues effectively, contributing to the successful execution of the testing process and the delivery of a software product that aligns with the expectations of the users and stakeholders. Get ready to embrace the challenges and complexities of issue management and transform them into opportunities for improvement and success.

Chapter 7.1: Identifying and Classifying Issues

Testing, at its core, is an act of identification – recognising the discrepancies, errors, and shortcomings that impede the functionality, usability, or performance of a software product. While defects are the most commonly identified issues in this realm, the term 'issue' in a broader sense encompasses a wider range of problems that can emerge during the testing process, such as challenges with the test environment, test data inaccuracies, or obstacles in the test execution process.

The journey of issue management begins with vigilant identification. It's a careful process of observation, understanding the software's expected behaviour, and juxtaposing it against the actual behaviour. A keen eye for detail and a deep understanding of the software application are vital assets for this task. It involves scrutinising every feature, every functionality, and every element of the user interface to ensure it behaves as expected. It also involves staying alert to issues outside the software itself, such as unexpected outcomes in the test environment or inconsistencies in the test data.

After identifying the issues, they must be accurately documented. Detailed and clear documentation is vital to ensure the right steps are taken to address the issues. Documentation typically includes a description of the issue, the steps to reproduce it, its observed and expected outcomes, and any other relevant information such as screenshots or log files.

The subsequent stage involves classifying the identified issues. This is a crucial process that lays the foundation for effective issue management. Classification helps in understanding the nature of the issue, its severity, and the urgency to resolve it.

Issues are typically classified based on their nature - whether they are defects in the software, problems in the test environment, or inaccuracies in the test data. Each of these categories may warrant different approaches for resolution, involving different teams or resources.

Severity classification pertains to the impact of the issue on the software's functionality or performance. A high-severity issue might render a critical functionality unusable, while a low-severity issue might be a minor discrepancy in the user interface that doesn't hinder the user's experience significantly.

Prioritisation of issues is another aspect of classification. Priorities are usually determined by the severity of the issue, its impact on the user, and its relevance to the current development or testing objectives. High-priority issues are typically those that require immediate attention due to their significant impact on the software or the project timeline.

The process of identifying and classifying issues, though demanding, is a cornerstone of issue management. It's the first step towards resolving these issues and ensuring the delivery of a quality software product. As we navigate through this process, we not only uncover the problems that mar our software but also unearth opportunities to improve it, making it more robust, reliable, and resonant with the user's needs. Remember, the goal isn't just to find problems but to facilitate solutions, and this journey starts with the crucial task of identifying and classifying issues.

Chapter 7.2: Managing Issue Resolution

The second phase of issue management, following identification and classification, is the process of resolution. It requires an in-depth understanding of the issue at hand, a logical approach to address it, and efficient coordination among the teams involved. In this stage, the role of a test manager expands from merely identifying issues to actually driving the steps towards their resolution.

Resolving issues starts with an analysis of each problem to understand its root cause. This involves re-visiting the documentation, reproducing the issue, and analysing its context. For software defects, this could mean understanding the code segments responsible for the anomaly. For test environment issues, it might involve reviewing the environment setup and configurations. And for test data discrepancies, it could imply scrutinising the data sets used. Each issue type demands a unique approach to its root cause analysis.

Once the root cause is identified, the test manager must decide on the resolution strategy. This usually involves consulting with relevant stakeholders, like the development team for software defects, the infrastructure team for test environment issues, or the test analysts for test data problems. Collaborative decision-making helps in ensuring that the resolution strategy is practical, efficient, and agreed upon by all parties involved.

The implementation of the resolution strategy often involves delegating tasks to different teams or individuals. As a test manager, one needs to ensure that these tasks are clearly communicated, properly understood, and promptly executed. Efficient delegation and communication are crucial to prevent any confusion or delays in issue resolution.

Monitoring the resolution process forms a significant part of this phase. It involves tracking the progress of resolution tasks, ensuring they are being carried out as planned, and intervening if there are any bottlenecks or delays. Regular status updates from the teams involved aid in this monitoring process.

The resolution process culminates with the verification of the issue fix or solution. This usually involves re-testing the resolved issue to confirm that it has been appropriately addressed and no longer persists. If the issue still persists, the resolution process may need to be re-visited.

The journey from identifying an issue to witnessing its resolution is a challenging one, requiring not just technical acumen but also project management skills, decision-making abilities, and adeptness at team coordination. However, as each issue finds its resolution, it brings along a sense of accomplishment, marking another step towards delivering a software product that meets the quality standards and user expectations. As test managers, we not only resolve issues but also build the bridges that connect problems to their solutions, marking the path towards a better software product.

Chapter 7.3: Reporting and Communicating about Issues

Communication and reporting are critical elements of issue management. They bridge the gap between identification and resolution, connecting the people, processes, and information involved. For a test manager, mastering these aspects is crucial to ensure effective issue management, keeping everyone informed and engaged throughout the process.

Communication about issues begins as soon as they are identified. This communication is typically targeted towards the individuals or teams responsible for the issue's resolution, such as the developers, system administrators, or database managers. The communication must clearly describe the issue, including its symptoms, reproduction steps, and any other pertinent details. This information, usually documented in an issue tracker, forms the basis for the resolution process. The test manager plays a key role in ensuring that this communication is accurate, clear, and promptly delivered.

Communication is not a one-time event but a continuous process throughout the issue's life cycle. Regular updates about the status of the issue's resolution, any challenges encountered, and revised estimates for completion are crucial to keep all stakeholders informed. This ongoing communication helps to set expectations, facilitates collaboration, and keeps everyone involved on the same page.

While communication is the dialogue surrounding the issues, reporting is the narrative. Reporting typically targets a wider audience, including not just the technical teams but also the project managers, business analysts, and even the clients. Therefore, it requires a more formal, structured, and comprehensive approach.

Issue reports typically provide a snapshot of the issue landscape, covering aspects such as the number of open issues, their severity and priority distribution, their status in terms of resolution, and any trends or patterns observed. They can also include insights from the issue data, such as areas of the software with the most issues, the most common types of issues, or the average time to resolve issues. These insights can be invaluable in guiding future testing efforts, improving the software quality, and enhancing the testing process itself.

The test manager is often responsible for preparing and presenting these reports. This task requires not just an understanding of the issue data but also the ability to analyse it, interpret it, and present it in a manner that is meaningful and useful to the audience. The use of visual aids such as charts, graphs, or tables can be instrumental in making the reports more comprehensible and impactful.

Communicating and reporting about issues is a vital responsibility of a test manager, connecting the dots in the issue management process. It involves speaking the language of the developers, resonating with the needs of the project managers, and aligning with the expectations of the clients. It's an art that transforms data into insights, uncertainties into expectations, and challenges into opportunities.

CHAPTER 8: QUALITY ASSURANCE AND CONTROL

In a world where the demand for high-quality software products is growing exponentially, the role of a test manager extends far beyond identifying and resolving issues. It reaches the realm of ensuring the software's quality from a holistic perspective, encompassing all stages of its lifecycle, from planning to deployment. This perspective involves implementing quality assurance practices, employing quality control techniques, and fostering a quality culture within the organisation. These components form the foundation of Chapter 8, a comprehensive look into Quality Assurance and Control.

Quality Assurance (QA) focuses on the software development process, seeking to prevent defects before they occur. As a proactive approach, it ensures that the process used to create the software is robust and efficient. This chapter will delve into "Implementing Quality Assurance Practices," discussing the application of standards, procedures, and guidelines that enhance the software development process. We will explore the role of a test manager in embedding QA into the day-to-day operations, providing a roadmap for teams to follow to create a quality product.

Quality Control (QC), on the other hand, is a reactive approach. It aims at identifying and fixing defects in the software product, ensuring that it meets the defined quality standards. In "Quality

Control Techniques," we will examine the tools and techniques that a test manager can employ to monitor the output of the software development process. These techniques act as a safety net, catching any issues that might have slipped past the QA measures.

However, QA and QC are not enough to assure software quality on their own. The secret sauce that binds them together and amplifies their effectiveness is a quality culture. A quality culture refers to an organisational environment where everyone, from developers to managers, values quality and contributes towards achieving it. "Building a Quality Culture" will discuss the role of a test manager in fostering such a culture. We will understand how to instil a mindset of quality, promote a spirit of teamwork, and empower every team member to contribute towards the quality goals.

Quality Assurance and Control is not just a chapter in the book of software testing; it is a philosophy that governs the entire narrative. It represents a shift from merely testing for defects to proactively preventing them, from merely reacting to quality issues to creating an environment where they are less likely to occur. It's about equipping a test manager with a compass that points towards quality, a lens that focuses on quality, and a language that speaks quality. As we embark on this journey of exploration into Quality Assurance and Control, remember that quality is not just a destination; it's a journey that starts with a commitment and culminates in customer satisfaction. Let's get started on this quality journey.

Chapter 8.1: Implementing Quality Assurance Practices

Quality Assurance (QA) is a vital facet of the software development process. As a proactive approach, it aims to instil quality right from the early stages, focusing on preventing defects before they occur. It ensures that the processes employed in the software's development are robust, efficient, and most importantly, consistent.

QA is not just about establishing standards and procedures; it's about ensuring their adherence throughout the software development lifecycle. It involves regular reviews and audits of the processes, identifying any deviations, and implementing corrective actions to bring them back in line. This continuous monitoring and improvement is what distinguishes QA from a one-time activity, making it a recurring theme in the software development symphony.

The first step in implementing QA practices is the establishment of process standards. These standards provide a framework for how the different tasks in the software development process should be performed. They outline the steps to be followed, the inputs to be used, the outputs to be produced, and the criteria to be met. These standards could be based on industry best practices, regulatory requirements, or organisational policies. However, they should be flexible enough to adapt to the changing needs of the project and the team.

The next step is to establish procedures that operationalise these standards. Procedures are detailed instructions that guide the team on how to perform the tasks according to the standards. They should be clear, concise, and easy to follow, minimising the scope for errors or misunderstandings. Creating comprehensive documentation for these procedures is essential to ensure their successful implementation. The documentation should be readily accessible to all team members, providing them with a valuable reference point for their tasks.

Once the standards and procedures are in place, the focus shifts to their adherence. This is where reviews and audits come in. Reviews involve examining the processes and their outputs to verify their compliance with the standards and procedures. They can be performed at different stages of the software development process, providing timely feedback, and allowing for early correction of deviations. Audits, on the other hand, are more formal and comprehensive evaluations performed at specific intervals. They provide an objective assessment of the process's adherence to the standards and procedures, identifying any gaps and recommending improvements.

However, QA doesn't stop at identifying and correcting deviations. It extends to analysing these deviations to understand their root causes. This analysis helps in identifying any systemic issues in the processes that could be leading to the deviations. Addressing these root causes prevents the recurrence of the deviations, leading to a sustained improvement in the process quality.

QA also involves continuous improvement of the processes. This involves not just addressing the identified issues but also proactively seeking opportunities to enhance the processes. It could be in terms of increasing their efficiency, improving their effectiveness, or enhancing their adaptability. The goal is to make the processes better with each iteration, driving the software quality upwards with each stride.

Implementing QA practices is an ongoing journey, a commitment to quality that permeates every aspect of the software development process. It requires a thorough understanding of the processes, an eye for detail to spot deviations, and a visionary mindset to envisage improvements. And as a test manager, it's a journey that you lead, guiding your team towards a destination where quality is not just an aspiration; it's a habit.

Chapter 8.2: Quality Control

Techniques

Quality Control (QC) is the counterpart to Quality Assurance, forming the other half of the quality management dyad. While Quality Assurance focuses on the processes to prevent defects, Quality Control is concerned with identifying and fixing defects in the software product itself. It's a reactive process that inspects the output of the software development process to ensure it meets the established quality standards.

Several techniques can be employed in Quality Control, each with its unique advantages. A robust QC approach often involves a blend of these techniques, carefully chosen based on the context of the project, the nature of the software product, and the specific quality requirements.

One of the fundamental techniques is code review, also known as peer review. It involves systematically examining the source code to detect and fix errors overlooked during the initial development phase. This method not only corrects mistakes but also promotes knowledge sharing among team members and encourages adherence to coding standards.

Another commonly employed technique is static analysis. It is an automated review of the source code without executing it. Static analysis tools scan the code to identify any potential issues, such as syntax errors, unused variables, memory leaks, or security vulnerabilities. These tools can be configured to align with the project's coding standards, making them an effective means of ensuring code quality.

On the other hand, dynamic analysis involves analysing the software during its execution. It identifies issues that may not be evident in the source code but become apparent when the software is running. These include performance issues, concurrency issues, or security vulnerabilities that manifest during operation.

Then there is functional testing, which verifies that the software performs as expected according to the defined requirements. It involves creating test cases based on the software's functionality and executing them to confirm the software's behaviour aligns with the expectations. Functional testing can be performed at different levels, from unit testing individual components to system testing the entire software.

Non-functional testing is another key QC technique, focusing on aspects like performance, usability, security, compatibility, and reliability. These factors contribute significantly to the user experience and are thus vital for the software's success. Non-functional testing involves creating specific test scenarios that simulate real-world usage conditions, providing a realistic assessment of the software's quality.

Finally, there's regression testing, which ensures that the software continues to function correctly after modifications. Whenever changes are made to the software, be it to fix defects or add new features, there's a risk that they might impact the existing functionality. Regression testing mitigates this risk by re-testing the affected parts of the software, confirming that the changes have not introduced any unintended side effects.

Implementing these Quality Control techniques requires a deep understanding of the software, a clear definition of the quality standards, and a meticulous approach to testing. It involves striking a balance between the different techniques, ensuring comprehensive coverage without compromising efficiency. And while it's a demanding role, the rewards are profound, contributing significantly to the software's quality, the customer's satisfaction, and ultimately, the project's success.

Chapter 8.3: Building a Quality Culture

Building a culture of quality within your team is no small task. It requires a change in perspective, a shift from viewing quality as merely an output to seeing it as an inherent aspect of every process and interaction. The goal is to make quality the responsibility of everyone on the team, transcending job titles and task assignments.

Cultivating a quality culture begins with leadership. As a test manager, your actions, attitudes, and expectations will significantly influence your team's approach to quality. Emphasise the importance of quality in your communications, reward quality-focused behaviour, and demonstrate a personal commitment to quality in your actions. Create an environment where everyone feels accountable for the quality of their work and understands how their role contributes to the overall quality of the product.

Training is another critical component of a quality culture. Ensure that all team members are equipped with the knowledge and skills necessary to perform their tasks to the highest standard. Provide regular training sessions on quality standards, best practices, and the use of quality tools. Moreover, encourage a learning culture where team members feel empowered to seek knowledge and improve their skills continually.

Communication plays a crucial role in fostering a quality culture. Encourage open and honest dialogue about quality issues and challenges. Facilitate regular meetings where team members can discuss their work, share their experiences, and learn from each other. Promote transparency and feedback, ensuring that everyone feels comfortable expressing their views and suggestions.

In addition to these, create processes that support quality. Implement quality checks at every stage of the software development lifecycle, from requirement gathering to deployment. Establish clear quality standards and use metrics to measure your team's performance against these standards. However, be wary of relying too heavily on metrics as they can sometimes lead to a focus on quantity over quality. Remember, the goal is to enhance quality, not just to meet numerical targets.

Institutionalise quality by integrating it into your team's daily activities. Encourage practices such as peer reviews, pair programming, and continuous integration, which promote collaboration and shared ownership of quality. Make quality an inherent part of your team's workflow, rather than an additional task or an afterthought.

Promoting a culture of quality also means dealing effectively with quality issues when they arise. Develop a proactive approach to problem-solving, focusing on root cause analysis rather than quick fixes. Encourage a mindset of continuous improvement, viewing mistakes as opportunities to learn and improve.

Lastly, remember that building a quality culture is a journey, not a destination. It requires patience, persistence, and a willingness to continually reassess and refine your approach. It might be challenging at times, but the rewards - in terms of enhanced product quality, improved customer satisfaction, and a more engaged and motivated team - are well worth the effort.

Remember, quality is not just about meeting specifications or passing tests. It's about creating software that meets the user's needs, delivers value, and creates a positive user experience. And this is what a culture of quality seeks to achieve. As a test manager, your role is to lead this cultural transformation, guiding your team on the path to quality excellence. And while the path may be long and arduous, the journey is one of growth, learning, and ultimately, fulfilment.

CHAPTER 9: TEST AUTOMATION MANAGEMENT

The advent of test automation has been a game-changer in the software testing domain. It has significantly expedited the testing process, reduced human error, and enabled more comprehensive coverage of the test space. However, implementing and managing test automation requires a unique blend of skills, knowledge, and strategies. This chapter delves into the sphere of test automation management, the pivotal role it plays in today's testing landscape, and how a test manager can efficiently oversee its implementation.

Understanding when to automate testing is often the first hurdle to cross. Not all tests are suitable or economically feasible for automation. This chapter will cover the factors to consider when deciding to automate, such as the repetitiveness of tests, their complexity, the required speed of feedback, and the lifecycle stage of the application under test. Furthermore, we will delve into how the return on investment (ROI) can guide your automation decisions and how to balance automated testing with manual efforts for optimal results.

Overseeing the implementation of test automation is a multifaceted task. Test managers need to coordinate with various stakeholders, manage resources, and ensure alignment with overall testing and business objectives. We will explore how a test manager can handle these responsibilities effectively. This involves selecting the appropriate automation tools, defining a robust automation strategy, handling the technical aspects of test automation, and overseeing the automation team's work. We will also explore how to manage the common challenges associated with test automation, such as maintaining the relevance and effectiveness of automation efforts as the software evolves.

Managing and maintaining test automation artifacts is a crucial but often overlooked aspect of test automation management. Test scripts, data, and outcomes need to be effectively managed to ensure the long-term success of test automation efforts. The chapter will delve into how to manage these artifacts, including version control, documentation, and the maintenance of automated test scripts. We will discuss best practices for managing these artifacts and how to adapt these practices as the software and the testing landscape evolve.

The dynamics of test automation management are as complex as they are critical. The transition from manual to automated testing is not just about using new tools or writing scripts. It is a transformational process that requires strategic planning, a keen understanding of your testing landscape, and effective management skills. As a test manager, you are the torchbearer of this transformation. This chapter will arm you with the knowledge and insights to guide your team through this journey and towards a future of efficient, effective, and successful automated testing.

Chapter 9.1: Understanding When to Automate

The decision to automate testing is an integral part of any test management strategy. While test automation can offer significant advantages, it's crucial to realise that it is not a cure-all solution. Misapplied automation can lead to unnecessary complexity, wasted resources, and could even compromise the quality of your testing process. Thus, understanding when to automate is of paramount importance.

The first consideration is the nature of the test cases. Repetitive tests that need to be executed multiple times over a considerable period are prime candidates for automation. They are typically time-consuming when performed manually, making them both tedious and prone to human error. Examples include regression tests, smoke tests, and sanity tests, which ensure that the existing functionalities of the software continue to work as expected after modifications.

The lifecycle stage of the application also impacts the decision to automate. In the initial phases of development, when the software is still prone to frequent changes, automated testing can be less effective due to the high maintenance cost of the test scripts. As the application matures and stabilises, the cost-benefit ratio of automation improves significantly. However, for certain types of testing like unit testing, automation is beneficial even during the early stages of development.

The complexity of the test cases is another crucial factor. Simple test cases with clear input-output relationships are generally suitable for automation. However, complex test scenarios that require sophisticated logic or human judgement may not be ideal for automation. For instance, exploratory testing, usability testing, and other tests involving subjective evaluations are generally better conducted manually.

Speed of feedback is another essential consideration. In today's agile and DevOps environments, rapid feedback is critical. Automated tests can provide fast, consistent results, enabling quicker identification and resolution of issues. Automated unit tests, for example, can provide immediate feedback to developers, enabling them to fix issues at an early stage, thus enhancing efficiency.

Moreover, the decision to automate should always be guided by a thorough cost-benefit analysis. Test automation involves significant upfront costs including tool acquisition, infrastructure setup, and script development and maintenance. These costs should be weighed against the expected benefits such as reduced execution time, improved accuracy, increased test coverage, and the ability to run tests more frequently. A return on investment (ROI) approach can help make this decision more objective and quantifiable.

It's vital to remember that a balance between manual and automated testing often yields the best results. Manual testing allows for human intuition and creativity, catching issues that might be missed by automated tests. On the other hand, automated tests offer speed, precision, and repeatability. A judicious combination of both approaches allows for thorough coverage, increased efficiency, and a robust testing process.

As a test manager, your role is to guide your team through these considerations, ensuring that the decision to automate is made thoughtfully and strategically. With a balanced, informed approach, test automation can be a powerful tool in your testing arsenal, driving efficiency and enhancing the overall quality of your software products.

Chapter 9.2: Overseeing the Implementation of Test Automation

Implementing test automation in an organisation is not merely a shift in the mechanics of testing, but a transformative process that impacts people, procedures, and objectives. As a test manager, overseeing this transition requires a keen understanding of the strategic alignment, technical intricacies, and organisational dynamics involved in automation.

A crucial first step is the selection of the right automation tools. Various tools cater to different needs – from unit testing and API testing to UI testing and load testing. Each tool has its unique strengths, features, and limitations. Moreover, the chosen tool should align with your team's skills and the technical architecture of the application under test. A thorough comparative analysis based on factors such as ease of use, script maintenance, reporting capabilities, integration with other tools, and cost can guide you towards the appropriate choice.

Once the tool is selected, defining a clear automation strategy is essential. This involves identifying which test cases to automate based on the considerations discussed in the previous section, determining the scope of automation, and outlining the automation process. At this stage, it's important to manage expectations realistically - understand that automation will not eliminate all bugs or reduce manual testing efforts to zero overnight. Instead, it should be viewed as a strategic long-term investment aimed at enhancing overall testing efficiency and effectiveness.

Handling the technical aspects of test automation is another critical responsibility. This includes overseeing the development and maintenance of test scripts, managing the test data and environment, and ensuring the quality and reliability of automated tests. As the tests will be run frequently and possibly by different testers, following good coding practices, adding appropriate comments, and maintaining a well-organised, modular structure for the test scripts is essential.

A significant part of overseeing the implementation involves managing the automation team's work. The transition from manual testing to automation may necessitate reskilling or upskilling of the team members. As a manager, you need to facilitate this learning process, offer necessary support, and ensure a smooth transition. In addition, regular review of the automated test results and the quality of the scripts, as well as addressing any issues or challenges encountered by the team, falls under your purview.

The introduction of test automation can also stir a change in the organisation's testing culture and dynamics. Resistance to change, especially when it involves learning new skills or tools, is a common human tendency. However, as a test manager, you can play a pivotal role in managing this change. Communication plays a vital role here – explaining the benefits of automation, how it would impact the team, and what it means for each member can alleviate apprehensions and foster acceptance.

Overseeing the implementation of test automation is a journey laden with challenges and opportunities. It requires strategic planning, technical acumen, management skills, and most importantly, a visionary approach that looks beyond the immediate hurdles and towards the potential benefits that effective automation can bring. Embracing this responsibility prepares you to lead your team confidently into the future of software testing, where automation will be a key driver of success.

Chapter 9.3: Managing and Maintaining Test Automation Artifacts

In the sphere of test automation, an artifact is a by-product or residue that provides valuable insight into the testing process. These artifacts include automation scripts, test data, test results, logs, and reports, each of which plays a pivotal role in the effectiveness of your automation strategy.

Managing automation artifacts begins with organising the scripts. As the library of automated test cases grows, their organisation can quickly become a daunting task. However, this can be mitigated by employing a well-structured, modular approach from the outset. Group test cases based on their functionality or the application module they relate to. Employ naming conventions that clearly indicate the purpose of the script, making it easier to locate, understand, and modify the scripts when necessary.

Maintaining test data is another essential aspect of artifact management. Automated tests often require specific sets of data to validate different scenarios. Managing this data effectively ensures that the right test conditions can be set up efficiently. The data should be stored securely and structured in such a way that it can be easily loaded and used by the automation scripts. Consider using tools or techniques for creating, managing, and disposing of test data systematically.

Another pivotal artifact in test automation is the test environment, which must be effectively managed to ensure reliable test execution. This involves setting up the necessary hardware and software, configuring the system settings, and managing access rights. In addition, you need to maintain the environment's stability, ensure its readiness before each test execution, and handle environment-specific issues promptly.

Next, comes the management of logs and reports. These artifacts contain valuable information about the test execution, including the success or failure of tests, error messages, and performance data. Effective log management involves establishing a systematic process for generating, storing, and analysing the logs. The logs should be designed to capture sufficient detail to aid in troubleshooting while avoiding unnecessary verbosity that might make them difficult to comprehend. On the other hand, the reports should present a concise, insightful summary of the test results, providing clear visibility into the state of product quality.

Artifact maintenance is a continuous process. Over time, the application under test evolves - new features are added, existing ones are modified, and some may become obsolete. Consequently, the automation artifacts, particularly the scripts and test data, must be regularly updated to stay in sync with the application. Regular reviews and updates of the artifacts are essential to maintain their relevance and effectiveness.

Managing and maintaining test automation artifacts is a critical task that ensures the longevity and effectiveness of your automation effort. It demands meticulous organisation, continuous monitoring, and regular updates. Despite the inherent challenges, effective management of these artifacts leads to higher efficiency, better control, and enhanced visibility into the testing process, ultimately enabling you to harness the full potential of test automation.

CHAPTER 10:

STAKEHOLDER

COMMUNICATION AND

REPORTING

Effective communication is not just about conveying information. It's about building trust, fostering understanding, and driving action. As a test manager, you play a crucial role in bridging the gap between your testing team and the broader organisation. The way you communicate and report your team's efforts can significantly impact project outcomes, stakeholder relationships, and overall team morale.

This chapter focuses on the art and science of stakeholder communication and reporting. Throughout my decade-long journey as a test manager, I've found that the ability to communicate effectively with a range of stakeholders – from developers, project managers, and senior leadership to clients and other external parties – is one of the most valuable and sought-after skills in this role.

The first section, "Effective Communication Skills for Test Managers," covers foundational communication concepts and tools, as well as practical techniques for making your communication more impactful. We'll delve into the nuances of verbal and written communication, active listening, and giving and receiving feedback. Furthermore, we'll discuss how to tailor your communication to suit different stakeholders, taking into account their unique perspectives, expectations, and communication styles.

Next, in "Reporting Test Results to Stakeholders," we'll explore the nuts and bolts of creating clear, concise, and compelling test reports. These reports not only provide visibility into the testing process and outcomes but also inform decision-making at various levels of the organisation. We'll discuss the key components of an effective test report, different reporting formats, and how to use data visualisation techniques to make your reports more digestible and engaging. We'll also touch on the importance of timing and frequency in reporting, as well as how to adapt your reports based on the specific needs and preferences of your stakeholders.

Lastly, we'll tackle a topic that many find challenging but is inevitable in any workplace: "Handling Difficult Conversations and Conflicts." Whether it's addressing performance issues within your team, managing expectations with stakeholders, or dealing with disagreements and conflicts, these situations require tact, empathy, and assertiveness. We'll provide practical advice on how to approach these conversations, manage emotions (both yours and others'), and work towards a resolution that maintains relationships and drives positive change.

The knowledge and skills you'll gain from this chapter are not just applicable within the confines of test management. They are fundamental life skills that will enhance your interactions and relationships, both professionally and personally. Remember, communication is not a one-way street, and it goes beyond just speaking and writing. It involves listening, understanding, and responding. It's about creating a dialogue that fosters mutual understanding, respect, and collaboration.

By the end of this chapter, you'll have a deeper understanding of the power and potential of effective communication and reporting in your role as a test manager. Let's embark on this journey towards becoming not just a better test manager, but a better communicator and leader.

Chapter 10.1: Effective Communication Skills for Test Managers

Communication is the linchpin that holds the wheel of any organisation together, and as a test manager, it is an essential skill you must hone. It's not just about the transmission of information - it's about fostering understanding, collaboration, and action.

Fundamentally, communication in a testing context serves two primary purposes: facilitating the work of the testing team and reporting on that work to relevant stakeholders. Striking a balance between these functions necessitates versatility in communication styles and methods.

The first step in effective communication is clarity. A vague instruction or ambiguous feedback can lead to confusion, inaccuracies, and rework. Be explicit and articulate in your communication, ensuring that your instructions, expectations, and feedback are comprehensible and actionable. Strive for simplicity and directness, avoiding unnecessary jargon and complexity. It's equally important to encourage and welcome questions, as they indicate engagement and the pursuit of clarity.

Active listening is another vital skill in the repertoire of a successful test manager. It involves fully concentrating, understanding, and responding to your conversation partner, demonstrating that you value their input and fostering an open dialogue. When your team members feel heard and understood, they're more likely to contribute ideas, voice concerns, and take ownership of their work.

Giving and receiving feedback constructively is an art that can significantly enhance the performance and dynamics of your testing team. When giving feedback, focus on behaviours and actions rather than personal traits. Make your feedback specific, timely, and balanced, combining praise for good work with constructive suggestions for improvement. When receiving feedback, view it as a gift for growth. Accept it graciously, ask clarifying questions if needed, and commit to addressing the areas highlighted for improvement.

Tailoring your communication to different stakeholders is crucial. Each stakeholder has unique interests, concerns, and communication preferences. Your team members might appreciate detailed technical discussions, while your senior leadership might prefer high-level summaries focusing on business impact. By understanding and respecting these differences, you can make your communication more effective and resonant.

Adapting your communication style based on the situation and the people involved is also important. Sometimes, a formal written communication is required, while other times, an informal face-to-face conversation would be more effective. Developing an ability to navigate these different situations with aplomb is an invaluable skill.

One of the hallmarks of a good communicator is the ability to facilitate productive meetings. As a test manager, you'll often lead meetings with different objectives, such as project kick-offs, status updates, issue resolution discussions, and retrospective reviews. Plan your meetings carefully, set clear objectives, manage the discussion to stay on track, and ensure everyone's voices are heard. Summarise the key points, decisions, and action items at the end to ensure everyone is on the same page.

Never underestimate the power of non-verbal communication. Your body language, eye contact, facial expressions, and tone of voice can speak volumes. They can affirm the sincerity of your words, demonstrate your engagement, and respect for others, and help build rapport and trust.

The journey towards becoming an effective communicator is ongoing. It requires self-awareness, practice, and a willingness to learn and adapt. Remember, the goal is not to be a perfect communicator, but a communicator who makes a positive impact on the team's performance, stakeholder relationships, and overall project success. It's about fostering a dialogue that promotes mutual understanding, collaboration, and progress.

Chapter 10.2: Reporting Test Results to Stakeholders

The reporting of test results is a critical aspect of any testing process. It's the lens through which stakeholders view the progress and quality of a product, thus influencing critical decision-making. Mastering the art of reporting not only entails providing accurate, comprehensive, and timely information but also presenting it in a way that is relevant and accessible to each stakeholder.

The first step to effective reporting is understanding your audience. Each stakeholder has unique informational needs and preferences, determined by their role, responsibilities, and their proximity to the project. For example, a developer might need detailed error reports and logs to fix bugs, a product manager might be interested in the overall product quality and the impact on the user experience, and a CEO might want to know how the testing progress aligns with business goals and timelines. By tailoring your reports to each stakeholder's needs, you ensure your communication is valuable and actionable.

The content of your reports should be driven by the principle of transparency. It's essential to report not just the successes but also the setbacks and challenges encountered during testing. Highlighting the issues uncovered, the risks they pose, and the recommended course of action demonstrates your team's commitment to quality and helps stakeholders make informed decisions. However, remember that transparency is not about overwhelming stakeholders with raw data. It's about presenting pertinent information in a clear, concise, and understandable way.

Effective test reports often include elements such as an executive summary, a detailed test summary, a breakdown of defects by severity and priority, an overview of the test coverage, the status of bug fixes, and a section on risks and issues. Remember, though, that the best test report is not necessarily the one that includes the most data but the one that communicates the most valuable insights. Therefore, strive to convert your raw testing data into meaningful information, and your information into actionable insights.

Visualisation is a powerful tool in your reporting arsenal. Graphs, charts, tables, and other visual elements can convey complex data in a digestible format, facilitating quick comprehension and decision-making. For instance, a bar chart can quickly show the distribution of defects across various modules, and a burn-down chart can visualise the rate at which bugs are being discovered and resolved.

When you're reporting on ongoing testing efforts, it's essential to provide regular updates, maintaining a rhythm that aligns with your stakeholders' needs. However, while routine is crucial, don't wait for the scheduled reporting times if you uncover a major issue. The value of test reporting lies in its ability to inform timely decision-making.

On a final note, don't overlook the power of narrative. Storytelling can make your reports more engaging and persuasive. Instead of just presenting the numbers, tell the story behind them. Why did a particular testing phase take longer than expected? How did an unforeseen issue affect the testing progress, and how did the team overcome it? What does the trend in the defect discovery rate indicate about the product quality? By contextualising your data within a narrative, you make your reports more relatable and impactful.

In the realm of test reporting, your role as a test manager is not just that of a communicator, but also a translator and an interpreter. You translate the technical language of testing into the business language of impact and value, and you interpret raw data to extract meaningful insights. By doing so, you bridge the gap between the testing team and the stakeholders, facilitating understanding, collaboration, and successful decision-making.

Chapter 10.3: Handling Difficult Conversations and Conflicts

In a fast-paced, high-pressure environment like software testing, difficult conversations and conflicts are almost inevitable. They might arise from disagreements about the scope of testing, the interpretation of results, or the way forward when an issue is uncovered. As a test manager, part of your responsibility is to handle these challenging situations with grace, empathy, and effectiveness.

A crucial aspect of dealing with difficult conversations is preparation. This starts with acknowledging the issue at hand, understanding the differing perspectives, and clarifying your own position. Often, difficult conversations involve complex emotions, high stakes, and a significant amount of uncertainty. By examining the situation from multiple angles, you build a balanced perspective and equip yourself to navigate the conversation constructively.

Timing and setting play a crucial role in shaping the outcome of a difficult conversation. Choose a time when all parties can engage without interruptions and in a neutral, comfortable setting. This physical and temporal space can help deescalate the emotional intensity and promote a focus on resolution.

Communication during difficult conversations should always strive to be clear, respectful, and honest. Begin by establishing a shared purpose for the conversation, whether it's resolving a conflict, exploring a difficult decision, or addressing an issue. Then, use "I" statements to express your perspective and feelings without blaming or criticising the other party.

For example, instead of saying, "You always dismiss our testing concerns", you might say, "I feel our testing concerns are not being fully considered." This approach reduces defensiveness and opens up space for mutual understanding.

Active listening is an invaluable skill in these situations. It involves fully focusing on the speaker, avoiding interruption, and responding thoughtfully. It signals respect for the other person's perspective and helps unearth underlying issues and emotions that might be fuelling the conflict.

Remember, the goal of these conversations is not to win an argument but to reach a mutually beneficial resolution. This involves a willingness to compromise, a commitment to maintaining the relationship, and a focus on the future rather than dwelling on past disagreements.

Sometimes, despite your best efforts, the conversation might not lead to a resolution, or it might even escalate the conflict. In such situations, it might be helpful to involve a neutral third party such as a senior manager or a HR representative. They can provide an outside perspective, mediate the discussion, and help guide towards a solution.

After a difficult conversation, it's essential to follow up. This might involve implementing the agreed-upon actions, monitoring the situation to ensure the conflict doesn't re-emerge, and providing support to the team as they navigate the aftermath. Following up not only helps cement the resolution but also rebuilds trust and strengthens relationships.

Handling difficult conversations and conflicts is undoubtedly challenging, but it's also an opportunity for growth – for you as a leader and for your team. It's a chance to demonstrate your commitment to fairness, respect, and open communication. It's a way to model resilience in the face of adversity and to foster a culture of constructive conflict resolution. And ultimately, it's a pathway to more robust, more collaborative, and more effective testing team.

CHAPTER 11:

CONTINUOUS

IMPROVEMENT IN TEST

MANAGEMENT

A key tenet of successful test management – and indeed, any area of business or project management – is the principle of continuous improvement. This involves a constant, systematic process of evaluating and refining practices, with an aim to make ongoing incremental enhancements that, over time, can lead to significant improvements in efficiency, effectiveness, and outcomes.

Continuous improvement in test management is not simply about making changes for the sake of change. It's about identifying what works and what doesn't, learning from both successes and failures, and implementing changes based on evidence and informed judgement. It's about creating a culture where the team is open to change and committed to constant learning and improvement.

In this chapter, we will delve deep into three critical aspects of continuous improvement in test management: post-release review and lessons learned, continual improvement practices, and staying updated with testing trends.

Post-Release Review and Lessons Learned: Any project's completion presents a valuable opportunity for reflection and learning. A post-release review allows the test team to take a step back and examine the testing process holistically – what went well, what didn't, and why. It's a chance to learn from the experiences and apply these lessons to future projects.

Continual Improvement Practices: Continual improvement is not a one-off task but an ongoing process. We'll look at how to embed continual improvement practices into your test management processes, including techniques like root cause analysis, process refinement, and feedback loops. We'll also delve into how data and metrics can drive improvement, offering insight into the areas of the testing process that are working efficiently and those that may need refinement.

Staying Updated with Testing Trends: As with any technological field, the world of software testing is continuously evolving. New methodologies, tools, and practices emerge; regulatory landscapes shift; user expectations change. To stay relevant and effective, it's crucial to keep pace with these trends. This section explores how to stay abreast of the latest developments in the testing field and how to discern which trends are worth integrating into your own practice.

Continuous improvement is an exciting journey, offering an opportunity to consistently build on past successes, learn from failures, and incrementally enhance the test management process. By fostering a culture of continual learning and adaptation, we can make sure our testing practices remain effective, relevant, and aligned with the changing demands of the software development landscape. This chapter aims to equip you with the tools, strategies, and mindset needed to embark on this journey and steer your testing team towards ever-higher standards of excellence.

Chapter 11.1: Post-Release Review and Lessons Learned

The concept of "Post-Release Review and Lessons Learned" centres on the principle of reflection. The point at which a project reaches completion is not simply the end of a journey; it also marks the beginning of a new one. It presents a vital opportunity for introspection, learning, and growth. The post-release review is where we transform our experiences – our successes, failures, challenges, and surprises – into invaluable insights that can shape our future endeavours and enhance our testing processes.

The first step in conducting a post-release review is to gather the team and stakeholders to discuss the project in retrospect. This meeting should not be a forum for finger-pointing or defensiveness; rather, it should be a safe space for open, honest dialogue. It's an opportunity for every participant to share their perspectives, to voice their thoughts on what went well and what didn't, and why. This diversity of input is invaluable. Different team members will have experienced the project from different angles, and their unique insights can help construct a holistic picture of the project's successes and shortcomings.

Once the discussion is complete, it's time to consolidate the feedback. The key here is to focus on the process, not individuals. The aim is to identify patterns and trends that can provide actionable insights. What aspects of the testing process were most effective, and why? Where did we encounter difficulties, and what underlying issues or obstacles contributed to these? Were there any unexpected outcomes, and what can we learn from these?

However, identifying these patterns is only the first half of the equation. The next step is to convert these insights into concrete, actionable plans for improvement. For example, if the review highlighted a consistent issue with test execution delays due to bottlenecks in the test environment setup, it may be beneficial to invest in infrastructure enhancements or adopt a more efficient test environment management strategy. If communication breakdowns were a recurring theme, we might need to review our communication protocols or invest in team building or communication skills training.

We must then translate these plans into specific, measurable, achievable, relevant, and time-bound (SMART) goals. Instead of saying, "We will improve our communication," we might aim to "Implement a weekly team sync-up meeting and a project communication tool by the start of the next project." By setting SMART goals, we make our plans for improvement tangible and trackable.

The process doesn't stop there. The real value of a post-release review comes from using it as a springboard for continuous improvement. This means not just implementing our improvement plans, but also monitoring their impact over time and refining them, as necessary. It means cultivating an ethos of continuous learning, where every project is seen as an opportunity to get better. It's about embracing a growth mindset, where challenges are not seen as failures, but as steppingstones towards greater efficiency and effectiveness.

The post-release review and lessons learned process is an investment. It requires time, effort, and commitment, and its benefits may not be immediately visible. But it's an investment that pays rich dividends in the long run. By systematically learning from our experiences and implementing improvements, we can significantly enhance our testing processes, deliver better outcomes, and create a stronger, more resilient testing team. It's a journey of ongoing growth – one that is both challenging and rewarding in equal measure.

Chapter 11.2: Continual Improvement Practices

In the dynamic world of software testing, stagnation equates to regression. Continual improvement is not just an aspirational goal; it's a vital necessity. A robust and progressive test management strategy recognises this need and integrates continual improvement practices at its core. These practices enable test teams to continuously refine their testing processes, methods, and tools, leading to higher quality software, more efficient testing, and a more engaged and capable team.

The first pillar of continual improvement practices is a commitment to learning. This commitment extends beyond just staying updated with the latest testing trends and technologies. It includes a proactive approach to acquiring new skills, embracing new methodologies, and understanding new paradigms that can enhance testing effectiveness. Training, workshops, webinars, conferences, and self-learning resources like books and online courses can all play a crucial role in this endeavour. Cross-training within the team can also be an effective strategy to share knowledge and foster a collaborative learning culture.

Another crucial aspect of continual improvement is the systematic identification and elimination of waste. 'Waste' in this context refers to any activity that consumes resources but does not add value to the testing process. This could include redundant test cases, unnecessary documentation, repetitive manual tasks that could be automated, or communication inefficiencies. Identifying and eliminating these wastes can dramatically streamline the testing process and free up resources for more valuable activities.

Continuous integration and delivery (CI/CD) practices are another valuable tool for continual improvement. CI/CD involves the frequent integration of code changes, automated testing of these changes, and seamless deployment to the production environment. By enabling rapid feedback on code quality and facilitating early detection of integration issues, CI/CD can significantly enhance testing efficiency and software quality.

Metrics and analytics are another crucial component of continual improvement practices. They provide the insights needed to understand the current state of the testing process, identify areas of concern, and track the progress of improvement initiatives. It's important, however, to choose meaningful metrics that align with the team's goals and provide value to the stakeholders. Common testing metrics include test coverage, defect density, defect resolution time, and test case effectiveness.

A key factor in implementing continual improvement practices is fostering a culture that supports and encourages improvement. This involves promoting a positive, open mindset where feedback is welcomed, mistakes are seen as opportunities for learning, and everyone is committed to improving their work. Regular retrospectives can facilitate this by providing a forum for the team to reflect on their work, discuss their challenges and successes, and brainstorm ideas for improvement.

An important principle to remember in implementing continual improvement practices is that improvement is a journey, not a destination. It involves small, incremental changes that accumulate over time to create significant results. It's not about pursuing the perfect testing process - because there's no such thing - but rather about constantly striving to make the existing process better. It's about acknowledging that no matter how well we're doing, we can always do better. And it's about recognising that every step we take on this journey - no matter how small - brings us one step closer to our goal of delivering the highest quality software in the most efficient and effective way possible.

Chapter 11.3: Staying Updated with Testing Trends

New technologies, methodologies, and tools are emerging at an astounding pace. New challenges and opportunities are continuously arising as the software landscape evolves. To stay effective and relevant in this dynamic environment, it is vital for test managers to stay updated with the latest testing trends.

One of the most significant trends in recent years has been the rise of agile and DevOps methodologies. These methodologies emphasise continuous integration, continuous testing, and rapid feedback, transforming the way testing is conducted. Testers are no longer isolated in a separate 'quality gate' phase but are integrated into the development team and involved throughout the software lifecycle. This trend towards closer integration and collaboration has significant implications for test management, from the way testing activities are planned and coordinated to the skills required in the testing team.

Another key trend is the increasing use of automation in testing. Test automation tools have become more sophisticated and powerful, capable of automating complex test scenarios and even generating test cases based on model or behaviour driven development. However, test automation is not a panacea and does not eliminate the need for manual testing. It's crucial to understand where automation can add value and where it can't, and to manage the balance between manual and automated testing effectively.

Artificial Intelligence (AI) and Machine Learning (ML) are also making their mark on the testing field. AI and ML can be used to predict high-risk areas for testing, generate and optimise test cases, and even identify defects in software without the need for explicit test cases. These technologies are still in their early stages, but they have the potential to revolutionise testing in the future.

Cloud computing and virtualisation are transforming the way test environments are managed. They enable test teams to quickly and easily spin up and tear down test environments as needed, reducing the overhead of environment management, and increasing flexibility. They also facilitate testing in realistic, production-like environments, enhancing the validity of test results.

The rise of mobile, IoT, and other distributed computing technologies has broadened the scope of testing. It's no longer sufficient to just test a software application in isolation. Testers need to consider the entire ecosystem in which the software operates, including diverse devices, operating systems, network conditions, and integration points. This has implications for the complexity and scale of testing activities, as well as the skills required in the test team.

Staying updated with these trends involves more than just reading articles or attending conferences. It involves a commitment to continuous learning and curiosity, a willingness to explore new ideas and challenge old assumptions. It requires a mindset of adaptability, flexibility, and openness to change.

However, it's also important to approach trends critically and thoughtfully. Not every trend will be relevant or beneficial for every situation. Some trends may be more hype than substance, or they may not align with the specific needs and constraints of your organisation. The challenge for test managers is to discern which trends are truly significant and beneficial, to understand how these trends can be applied in their specific context, and to lead their teams in adapting to these trends in a way that enhances the effectiveness and value of testing.

Ultimately, staying updated with testing trends is about positioning oneself and one's team to continue delivering value in a changing world. It's about being proactive rather than reactive, leading the change rather than just following it. It's about ensuring that testing continues to fulfil its essential role of assuring quality, reducing risk, and enabling the delivery of great software.

CHAPTER 12:

LEADERSHIP AND

PROFESSIONAL

DEVELOPMENT

We will now focus on two essential elements that intertwine and play a vital role in your success as a Test Manager: leadership and professional development. While technical competence and understanding of software testing are crucial, the more profound, more intangible aspects of leadership and continual growth often distinguish exceptional managers.

In this chapter, we will explore the importance of developing leadership skills as a test manager. A test manager's role goes beyond merely overseeing the testing process; it involves influencing, guiding, and developing a team. It's about nurturing a collaborative environment where individuals feel heard, valued, and motivated to contribute to the broader objectives. Moreover, being an effective leader also requires the ability to manage upwards and sideways - to communicate the value and needs of testing to other stakeholders in the organisation, and to navigate the political and cultural landscape of the organisation effectively. You'll learn strategies and techniques to hone these leadership skills and apply them in your daily work.

Next, we will delve into promoting professional development within your team. As a test manager, one of your key responsibilities is to foster an environment that encourages learning and development. This includes facilitating training and learning opportunities, encouraging knowledge sharing, providing constructive feedback, and nurturing the skills and career development of each team member. When a team is continuously learning and improving, it becomes more capable, versatile, and resilient. This section will provide practical advice on how to create and sustain such an environment.

Lastly, we'll discuss the importance of networking and influencing within the wider organisation. While the testing team plays a crucial role in any software development lifecycle, it's essential to remember that it is part of a larger whole. Effective test managers must be able to build positive relationships with other teams and departments, from developers and business analysts to project managers and executives. They must be able to advocate for the needs and perspectives of testing, influence decision-making, and contribute to broader organisational objectives. We will offer guidance on how to build these networks, navigate organisational dynamics, and wield influence effectively.

The threads of leadership and professional development run through every aspect of test management, from the way you interact with your team members and other stakeholders to the way you approach challenges and opportunities. As we traverse this chapter, the objective is to equip you with the insights and tools you need to elevate your leadership and drive professional development, both for yourself and your team. Whether you're an aspiring test manager, a newcomer to the role, or an experienced veteran, we hope this chapter will inspire you, challenge you, and guide you on your journey of growth and development in the fascinating field of test management.

Chapter 12.1: Developing Leadership Skills as a Test Manager

Technical proficiency alone doesn't suffice. As a Test Manager, the essence of your role merges with leadership, influencing your team's output and its members' personal growth trajectories. Leadership isn't a title; rather, it's a set of behaviours and practices that inspire, guide, and foster collaboration. Developing these leadership skills is an ongoing journey, one that starts with self-awareness and branches out to encompass communication, empathy, strategic thinking, and more.

One of the first steps towards effective leadership is understanding your leadership style and how it impacts your team. Are you more directive, instructing your team members on what to do, or more supportive, helping them find their solutions? There's no 'correct' style—each has its place. The key is to be adaptable, adjusting your approach to different people and situations.

Listening forms, a fundamental aspect of leadership. Often underemphasised, active listening can drastically enhance team dynamics. When your team feels heard and understood, they're more likely to contribute their thoughts and ideas, leading to more creative solutions and an engaged, invested team. Active listening also aids in identifying and resolving issues early, mitigating potential conflicts or misunderstandings.

Empathy complements listening. Understanding the feelings and perspectives of team members allows you to build stronger relationships and manage conflict more effectively. This includes understanding their career goals, personal circumstances, and their distinct working styles. Demonstrating empathy often leads to a more harmonious and productive team environment, where members feel understood and valued.

Strategic thinking is another critical leadership skill. As a Test Manager, you're not just managing the day-to-day operations of testing, but also strategising its future direction. You'll need to interpret broader organisational goals and devise strategies that align your team's work with these objectives. Moreover, you should be able to communicate this strategy to your team, ensuring everyone understands and works towards a common purpose.

Problem-solving and decision-making abilities also define a successful leader. Inevitably, issues will arise in testing, whether it's a difficult bug, a delayed schedule, or conflict within the team. Your ability to calmly assess the situation, generate possible solutions, make informed decisions, and take responsibility for the outcomes, is vital.

Developing leadership skills involves continual learning and self-improvement. This means seeking feedback, whether from your team, peers, or superiors, and using it to refine your leadership approach. It also involves staying updated on leadership trends, theories, and best practices. This can be achieved through reading, training courses, or mentoring relationships. Remember, even the most experienced leaders never stop learning and growing.

Cultivating these leadership skills requires patience, practice, and introspection. There will be mistakes along the way, and that's perfectly okay. It's these trials and errors, coupled with the willingness to learn, that mould you into a better leader. Throughout this journey, always remember that leadership in test management, or any field for that matter, is not about wielding power, but about empowering others. As you empower your team, foster their growth, and lead by example, you'll witness the transformative impact of strong leadership on your team's morale, productivity, and overall success.

Chapter 12.2: Promoting Professional Development within Your Team

As a Test Manager, promoting professional development within your team serves dual objectives. Not only does it equip your team members with the skills necessary to excel in their roles and tackle the complexities of evolving technologies, but it also fosters a culture of learning and growth, boosting morale and retention rates.

Setting the stage for professional development starts with creating an environment where learning is valued and encouraged. This includes communicating the importance of continual learning and recognising team members' efforts to acquire new skills or knowledge. It also entails integrating learning into the fabric of everyday work, fostering a culture where each task, project, or problem is viewed as an opportunity to learn and grow.

One practical strategy for promoting professional development is creating individualised learning paths. This begins with understanding each team member's current skill set, career aspirations, and areas they wish to develop. Based on this information, you can collaborate with them to craft a learning plan that aligns with their professional goals and the needs of the team. This could encompass a blend of on-the-job training, mentoring, online courses, or industry certifications.

Another critical component is fostering a feedback culture. Regular feedback gives your team members insight into their strengths, areas of improvement, and their progress towards their development goals. This feedback should be constructive and balanced, highlighting positives while offering actionable recommendations for improvement. Likewise, encourage team members to provide feedback to each other and to you as a manager. This facilitates a culture of open communication and continuous improvement.

Mentoring can also play a pivotal role in professional development. As a Test Manager, you can offer your experience and insights to help guide your team members' growth. Additionally, setting up a mentoring program within the team or the broader organisation can be highly beneficial. This not only allows less experienced team members to learn from their more experienced peers but also provides an opportunity for those in mentoring roles to develop their leadership and communication skills.

Learning opportunities should extend beyond the boundaries of the team or organisation. Encourage your team members to participate in industry conferences, seminars, and webinars. This exposure can provide them with insights into the latest testing trends, methodologies, and tools, fostering innovation and ensuring the team remains agile in the face of technological changes.

Similarly, support participation in professional networking groups or online communities. These platforms allow your team members to connect with industry peers, engage in discussions, and share knowledge.

Lastly, it's important to recognise and celebrate your team members' development milestones, whether it's completing a challenging project, acquiring a new certification, or demonstrating a newly learned skill effectively. This not only motivates them to continue their learning journey but also showcases the value your team places on growth and development.

Promoting professional development within your team is a dynamic, ongoing process. It requires commitment, adaptability, and a genuine interest in your team members' growth. Remember, by investing in your team's development, you're not only elevating their potential but also enriching the collective strength and future readiness of your team. It's this synergy between individual growth and team success that ultimately underpins the transformative power of professional development.

Chapter 12.3: Networking and Influencing in the Wider Organisation

A Test Manager plays a vital role in shaping the software testing landscape within an organisation. However, to realise the full potential of this role, it is essential to expand your reach beyond the confines of your team, to network and influence across the wider organisation. This is more than just a series of tactical manoeuvres; it is about weaving a narrative of collaborative success that resonates with various stakeholders, from the executive suite to the development floor.

Effective networking within an organisation is the art of fostering meaningful connections and partnerships. It's about creating an extensive web of relationships with individuals across departments and roles, founded on mutual respect and trust. It isn't merely about knowing people but rather about being known for your expertise, integrity, and ability to deliver value.

Begin your networking journey by understanding the organisation's landscape. Gain insights into different departments, their roles, challenges, and interdependencies. This knowledge allows you to tailor your communication effectively, bridging gaps and fostering cooperation.

An excellent way to initiate this process is through cross-departmental projects or initiatives. Participating in such endeavours provides an opportunity to collaborate with different teams, understand their perspectives, and demonstrate your ability to contribute to shared goals. This, in turn, helps you to establish credibility, paving the way for more influential relationships.

In the journey of networking and influencing, communication is your primary tool. It's crucial to articulate your ideas and insights clearly and persuasively, aligning them with the organisation's objectives and values. This helps you gain buy-in for your testing strategies and initiatives and ensures they are viewed as integral to the organisation's success.

A critical aspect of this communication is the ability to translate technical testing concepts into business language. This bridges the gap between the testing team and non-technical stakeholders, fostering understanding and collaboration. It enables you to highlight the value of testing efforts in terms that resonate with stakeholders, like product quality, customer satisfaction, or risk mitigation.

Active participation in organisational meetings, forums, or events can also amplify your influence. These platforms provide an opportunity to share your expertise, provide insights, and demonstrate your leadership. By engaging in these forums, you not only enhance your visibility but also position yourself as a thought leader, someone whose insights and opinions are sought and valued.

Influencing is not a one-way street. It's important to cultivate a listening mindset, welcoming ideas, feedback, and perspectives from others. This encourages open dialogue, promotes trust, and ensures that your influencing efforts are not perceived as mere self-promotion.

Building alliances with other leaders within the organisation can further boost your influencing efforts. Such alliances can provide you with insights, support, and additional avenues to effect change. Collaborating with these leaders on shared objectives can yield synergistic results, elevating the success of your team and the organisation.

Embody the values and behaviours you advocate. Your actions often speak louder than your words, and consistent, authentic actions can profoundly impact your influence within the organisation. This requires integrity, commitment, and a genuine desire to contribute to the organisation's success.

While networking and influencing might seem daunting, remember that it's a journey. Each conversation, each project, each shared success, takes you one step closer to becoming a more connected and influential Test Manager. By integrating networking and influencing into your role, you position yourself and your team as central contributors to the organisation's success story.

CHAPTER 13: TEST MANAGEMENT TOOLS AND TECHNOLOGIES

Our focus now pivots towards the technical aspects of test management, specifically addressing the crucial role of test management tools and technologies. In an age of rapid technological progression, mastering these tools and technologies is not just beneficial, it is a necessity. They are essential companions to the test manager, enhancing efficiency, reducing manual effort, providing insightful metrics, and aiding in strategic decision-making.

This chapter sets out to provide a comprehensive understanding of the popular tools available in the market, methods to evaluate and implement them, and guidelines to ensure their effective utilisation. It is about translating the wealth of your management knowledge into smart, technologically supported actions, leading your team to execute tests more accurately and productively.

In our first section, we delve into an overview of popular test management tools. The landscape of testing tools is rich and varied, encompassing a broad range of functionalities. You'll find tools designed for managing and tracking test cases, automated testing tools, performance testing tools, defect tracking systems, and more. Understanding their capabilities and how they can be leveraged is crucial in determining what would best suit your team and project needs.

We will then navigate towards evaluating and implementing these tools. The market is saturated with numerous tools, each with its unique blend of features, complexities, and learning curves. Selecting the right tool for your team requires careful consideration, not just of the tool's technical prowess, but also of factors such as cost, support, integration capabilities, and user-friendliness. Once the tool is selected, implementing it effectively is the next critical step. This phase is not just about technical installation, but also about configuring the tool to fit your processes, training the team, and managing the change effectively.

Our final section focuses on ensuring effective use of these tools. Procuring a powerful tool is just the start; the real benefits come from its optimal utilisation. This requires thorough knowledge of the tool's capabilities, continuous learning and updates, effective integration with other tools and systems, and regular review and feedback. You'll also learn about common challenges in tool usage and strategies to overcome them.

At the heart of this chapter lies a pivotal premise: Tools and technologies, when understood and used correctly, can be a significant force multiplier for a test manager. However, remember that tools are only enablers. They cannot replace a robust testing strategy, skilled team members, or effective management. Instead, they exist to amplify these elements, enabling you to manage your testing activities more efficiently and effectively.

As we traverse through this chapter, we hope to equip you with the knowledge and strategies to harness the power of test management tools and technologies effectively. It's about transitioning from just managing the tests to managing them smartly, leveraging technological advancements to drive your testing success to new heights.

Chapter 13.1: Overview of Popular Test Management Tools

The choice of the right test management tool can be instrumental in the efficiency and success of your testing processes. A tool that dovetails with your team's needs and work processes can enhance productivity, reduce manual effort, and provide valuable insights. Here we shall navigate through some of the popular tools that have made their mark in the test management landscape, aiding numerous test managers in their quest for quality and efficiency.

First in line is JIRA, a name that resonates prominently in the realms of issue tracking, project management, and, of course, test management. From the house of Atlassian, JIRA provides robust functionalities for tracking bugs and managing tasks. With its extension JIRA Test Management (JTM), it ventures into test case management, offering features like creation and management of test cases, linking tests with requirements, and traceability.

Next, we have TestRail, a comprehensive web-based test case management tool. It allows for managing, tracking, and organising software testing efforts efficiently. Key features of TestRail include managing test cases, planning and running tests, tracking results, comprehensive reporting, and integration with bug tracking tools. Its seamless integration capabilities with other software like JIRA make it a preferred choice for many teams.

Moving forward, we encounter Zephyr, a real-time test management tool providing end-to-end solutions for agile teams of all sizes. It integrates with JIRA, Confluence, and a host of other software, making it a versatile choice. Key features include creating, viewing, and editing test cases, comprehensive dashboards, advanced analytics, and execution tracking.

Micro Focus ALM/Quality Centre is another heavyweight in the test management tools arena. It offers end-to-end solutions, including requirements management, test planning, functional testing, and defect tracking. Its robustness and comprehensive coverage of testing lifecycle make it a popular choice among large organisations.

In the realm of open-source tools, one cannot overlook TestLink. It covers a range of features including test case creation and management, requirements specification, and test plan creation. Its open-source nature makes it an economical choice, particularly for small teams or startups.

Lastly, let's look at qTest, a tool that provides a suite of solutions to align with different stages of the testing lifecycle. It offers functionalities for test management, exploratory testing, test automation, and business-driven development. Its strong integration with various other tools like JIRA and automation tools adds to its appeal.

While we have only skimmed the surface, these tools are representative of the diverse offerings in the test management tools market. Each tool comes with its strengths, complexities, and learning curves. Understanding these tools' capabilities and how they can fit your needs is crucial in the tool selection process.

These tools, while invaluable, are constantly evolving, with new ones entering the market and existing ones undergoing updates and enhancements. This dynamic nature of the tools landscape makes it essential for test managers to stay updated, understanding not just the tools of today but also those on the horizon.

In the forthcoming sections, we will delve deeper into the process of evaluating these tools, implementing them in your work environment, and ensuring their optimal usage. But before we proceed, remember that the tool itself is not the solution, but an enabler. It should complement your testing strategy, dovetail with your team's skills, and enhance your team's efficiency and productivity. The right tool, in the right hands, with the right strategy, can be a potent force multiplier in your quest for testing excellence.

Chapter 13.2: Evaluating and Implementing Test Management Tools

The evaluation and subsequent implementation of test management tools demand thoughtful consideration. The task involves understanding the distinct needs of the organisation and the teams involved, comparing those needs against what each tool can offer, and finally, making the selection that will most effectively and efficiently meet the objectives at hand.

A fundamental consideration in the evaluation process is the alignment of the tool with the software development methodology in use within the organisation. For instance, an organisation that primarily adheres to Agile methodologies will require a tool that supports real-time collaboration, continuous integration, and has the flexibility to adapt to changing requirements.

Another significant factor is the ease of use of the tool. A tool may have a plethora of advanced features, but if it presents a steep learning curve, it may deter the team members from embracing it, leading to inefficient usage or even abandonment. Therefore, consider choosing a tool that balances sophistication with simplicity, ensuring that it can be effectively used by everyone on the team.

An often overlooked, but equally important, aspect is the tool's ability to integrate with other tools in the software development lifecycle. Seamless integration with requirements management tools, project management tools, version control systems, and Continuous Integration/Continuous Deployment (CI/CD) tools can make workflows smooth and efficient.

Finally, and perhaps most crucially, comes the question of budget. The cost of the tool is not confined to its purchase price but extends to training costs, maintenance costs, and upgrade costs. Balancing the budgetary constraints with the expected benefits from the tool is essential to making a financially sound decision.

Once the evaluation process concludes, and a decision has been made, the next step is implementing the chosen test management tool. This phase is pivotal as it lays the groundwork for how effectively the tool will be used in the future.

The implementation phase should start with a clear roadmap, setting out what needs to be achieved and within what timeframe.

This should be followed by a pilot phase where a small group of users can use the tool on a trial basis, testing its features, and providing feedback. This feedback is crucial for ironing out any issues before the tool is rolled out to the larger team.

Training forms a significant part of the implementation phase. It is imperative that all team members who will be using the tool receive adequate training. This training should cover not just the functionalities of the tool but also how those functionalities align with the team's work processes.

Lastly, the tool's implementation should be followed by a period of support and guidance where team members can seek assistance in case, they face any challenges in using the tool. This period is critical for ensuring that the tool is not just implemented but also accepted and used effectively by the team.

Choosing the right test management tool, evaluating its capabilities against your needs, and implementing it effectively can make a significant difference in your team's productivity and the quality of the end product. However, remember that the tool is only as good as the processes it enables and the people who use it. Therefore, in addition to focusing on the tool, pay equal attention to improving the processes and enhancing the skills of the team members.

Chapter 13.3: Ensuring Effective Use of Tools

The path to ensuring effective use of test management tools doesn't end at successful implementation. The true test lies in whether the tool gets used to its full potential, enhancing the team's efficiency and productivity. This chapter aims to provide a roadmap for ensuring that your team uses the tools effectively and optimally.

At the outset, cultivating a culture of openness towards new technologies and tools within your team is of paramount importance. Resistance to change is a common hurdle that often prevents the effective use of tools. Tackling this resistance head-on through open discussions about the benefits of the new tool, how it makes the work easier, and how it aligns with the team's goals can help in overcoming the initial reluctance.

Further, the successful adoption of a tool is closely linked with the adequacy of training provided to the users. It is imperative to ensure that all team members, regardless of their role, understand the functionalities of the tool and how to use it in the context of their work. Regular refresher training sessions can help keep the knowledge up-to-date and address any emerging issues.

Next, it's crucial to revisit and refine the processes that the tool is aiding. A tool, no matter how advanced, cannot replace a well-thought-out and streamlined process. Therefore, analyse the workflows and processes in your team regularly to ensure they are efficient and can leverage the tool's capabilities.

Also, it's important to remember that the goal of using a tool should not be to automate every single task. While automation can significantly boost productivity, there are aspects of testing that require human intuition, experience, and creativity. Striking a balance between automation and manual work can lead to more effective use of the tool.

Maintaining a strong line of communication with the tool vendor can also contribute to effective tool usage. Regular updates and upgrades can bring in new features that may be beneficial to your team. Moreover, tool vendors can provide valuable support in troubleshooting any issues that might arise, thus reducing downtime and enhancing efficiency.

Regularly monitoring and evaluating the use of the tool can provide insightful data about its effectiveness. Key performance indicators (KPIs) can be set up to measure the tool's impact on productivity, error rates, time to test, and other relevant aspects. If the tool doesn't seem to be delivering the expected results, it may be time to revisit your training and processes, or in some cases, consider a different tool.

Lastly, encouraging feedback from the users is a simple yet powerful way to ensure effective tool usage. This feedback can provide insights into the challenges the users are facing, the features they find most useful, and the improvements they would like to see. Such feedback can guide your decisions about future training, process changes, and tool upgrades.

When effectively used, test management tools can bring a transformation in the efficiency, productivity, and quality of your testing processes. However, ensuring effective use requires continual effort, adaptability, and a focus on people and processes, along with the tool itself.

CHAPTER 14:

NAVIGATING THE

FUTURE OF TEST

MANAGEMENT

The rapidly evolving field of software testing continues to shape and be shaped by innovations and trends in technology and software development methodologies. In this constantly changing landscape, effective test management is more crucial than ever. In this chapter, we will be navigating through the future of test management, focusing on emerging technologies and paradigms that are expected to influence this domain significantly.

Firstly, we'll delve into the impact of Artificial Intelligence (AI) and Machine Learning (ML) on test management. These ground-breaking technologies are revolutionising many aspects of our lives, and their potential in software testing is immense. AI and ML can enhance test automation, make sense of massive volumes of data, predict future trends, and much more. How can test managers harness these technologies to their advantage while mitigating associated risks and challenges? We'll seek to answer these questions in the first part of this chapter.

Next, we will navigate the shift in the landscape of software development methodologies that directly influence test management. Agile and DevOps have emerged as dominant approaches in the software industry, transforming the way teams develop and deliver software. What does this mean for test management? We will explore how test management fits into these environments, and how test managers can navigate the associated challenges and opportunities.

Preparing for future trends in test management will be our focus. Change is the only constant in the technology sector. New developments, be it in technology, methodologies, regulations, or customer expectations, will continue to influence how we manage testing. How can test managers stay ahead of the curve and prepare their teams for future trends? What skills and mindsets will be crucial in the test manager's toolkit as we move forward?

As we journey through this chapter, it is important to remember that while the future may bring many changes, the fundamental principles of test management remain. Ensuring software quality, effective communication, robust planning, and coordination, problem-solving, and continually learning and improving – these aspects will continue to be at the heart of test management.

Embracing the future of test management is not merely about adopting new technologies or methodologies. It's about cultivating a mindset of adaptability, lifelong learning, and proactive planning. It's about leading your team with confidence and competence through the uncertainties of the future. As we delve into these exciting topics, we hope this chapter will equip you with insights and strategies to navigate your path as a test manager in the dynamic future that lies ahead.

Chapter 14.1: The Impact of AI and Machine Learning on Test Management

The accelerating growth of Artificial Intelligence (AI) and Machine Learning (ML) in the technology sphere has introduced profound shifts across various industries. In the realm of software testing and test management, the potential of these technologies to create efficiencies and redefine existing procedures is significant. However, with this potential also comes the need to navigate new complexities and challenges.

AI and ML are capable of reshaping the testing landscape by automating complex tasks, analysing vast volumes of data, predicting trends, and even learning and improving over time. The most immediate impact of these technologies on test management is in the realm of test automation. Intelligent automation systems can now design and execute tests, understand the results, and even adapt and learn from each iteration. This reduces the manual effort, speeds up the testing cycle, and increases the coverage and accuracy of tests.

However, the benefits do not stop at efficiency gains. AI and ML can aid in decision making as well. By analysing vast amounts of test data, these technologies can generate insightful patterns and trends. This data-driven approach enables test managers to make more informed decisions about where to focus their testing efforts, which in turn enhances the effectiveness of the testing process.

Furthermore, predictive analytics, an application of AI, allows test managers to foresee potential issues and trends. For instance, predictive models can determine the areas of the software that are most likely to contain defects or indicate how modifications in the codebase could affect overall system stability. Armed with this information, test managers can proactively mitigate risks and optimise testing strategies.

On the other side of the coin, the introduction of AI and ML in test management also presents a new set of challenges. Implementing these technologies requires significant changes in the team's skillset. Testers need to understand how AI and ML tools work, interpret their output, and integrate them into the existing test environment. This may require substantial training and a shift in mindset.

Moreover, these technologies introduce new areas that need testing. AI and ML algorithms, due to their complex and often 'black box' nature, need specific testing strategies to ensure they function correctly and don't introduce unforeseen problems. As a result, test managers need to consider these factors when planning and coordinating testing activities.

Additionally, as with any new technology, AI and ML carry ethical and regulatory considerations. Their use in testing must be transparent, fair, and in line with privacy regulations. Hence, test managers must have an understanding of these aspects to ensure that their implementation of AI and ML in testing is both effective and responsible.

Therefore, while the advent of AI and ML in testing presents exciting opportunities for efficiency and insight, it also calls for careful navigation and proactive management. Embracing these technologies is not simply about adopting the latest tools, but rather about understanding their implications, adapting to their challenges, and leveraging them in a way that is beneficial and sustainable. The test manager, with their unique blend of technical, managerial, and strategic acumen, will play a crucial role in this journey.

Chapter 14.2: Test Management in Agile and DevOps Environments

methodologies like Agile and DevOps, emphasising rapid iterations, close collaboration, and continuous delivery. As these approaches become the norm, traditional test management strategies are evolving to keep pace.

In an Agile environment, where development and testing activities are intertwined and occur concurrently, the role of a test manager takes on new dimensions. Rather than overseeing testing as a distinct phase, the focus shifts to facilitating testing throughout the entire development lifecycle. This requires a mindset change: viewing testing not as a gatekeeper but as an integral part of the team's collective responsibility.

In such a setting, one of the crucial tasks is to ensure that testing activities align with Agile principles. This implies fostering a culture where everyone in the team understands and appreciates the value of testing. The practices of Test-Driven Development (TDD) and Behaviour-Driven Development (BDD) become essential tools in the test manager's toolbox, promoting a 'test-first' approach that integrates testing into the fabric of development.

Furthermore, the iterative nature of Agile demands that testing activities be flexible and adaptive. Test managers must be able to quickly refocus testing efforts based on feedback from each iteration or sprint. This requires effective prioritisation of testing tasks, taking into account the risk, value, and feasibility of testing different aspects of the system.

As Agile blurs the boundaries between development and testing, DevOps goes a step further and encompasses operations into the mix. In a DevOps environment, the goal is to achieve continuous integration and continuous deployment (CI/CD), making testing a continuous process. The challenge for test managers here is to ensure that testing does not become a bottleneck in the delivery pipeline.

To achieve this, test managers need to promote a high level of test automation, enabling fast and reliable execution of tests at each stage of the pipeline. They also need to facilitate effective communication and collaboration between development, testing, and operations teams to ensure that testing activities are well-integrated and do not disrupt the flow of the pipeline.

Moreover, in DevOps, monitoring and feedback become crucial sources of information for testing. By continuously monitoring the system in production and gathering feedback from users, test managers can gain valuable insights into how the system behaves in the real world. This data can inform and guide testing efforts, making them more relevant and effective.

Despite the unique challenges that Agile and DevOps present, they also offer significant opportunities for enhancing the value and impact of testing. By promoting a culture where everyone is involved in testing, by integrating testing activities throughout the development lifecycle, and by harnessing the power of automation, monitoring, and feedback, test managers can help their teams deliver software that is not just functional but also robust, reliable, and in tune with user needs.

In essence, managing testing in Agile and DevOps environments is about embracing change, fostering collaboration, and focusing on delivering value continuously. While it may require stepping out of comfort zones and challenging traditional notions of testing, the rewards - in terms of speed, quality, and satisfaction - are well worth the effort.

Chapter 14.3: Preparing for Future Trends in Test Management

As test managers, the responsibility lies not only in managing present circumstances but also in preparing for future shifts in the testing landscape. To navigate the ever-evolving terrain, one must develop a keen sense of foresight and flexibility.

As we look toward the horizon, one emerging trend is the increasing dominance of artificial intelligence (AI) and machine learning (ML) in testing. These technologies promise to revolutionise the way testing is performed and managed, enabling faster and more precise identification of defects, predicting potential areas of risk, and automating repetitive tasks.

Adapting to this future involves embracing AI and ML technologies and acquiring the skills needed to manage and utilise them effectively. This doesn't imply becoming AI experts but rather understanding the possibilities and limitations of these technologies and knowing how to integrate them into testing strategies.

Simultaneously, the move towards more integrated development practices, as seen in Agile and DevOps methodologies, is likely to continue. This implies the role of test management evolving from overseeing a distinct testing phase to facilitating a continuous and collaborative testing process. Therefore, test managers must develop competencies in these methodologies and learn to manage testing in a way that complements, rather than disrupts, the flow of the development pipeline.

On the horizon, we also see a growing emphasis on customer experience (CX) testing. As businesses strive to deliver exceptional digital experiences, testing will need to go beyond functionality and performance to encompass every aspect of the user experience. This shift requires a broader perspective on what constitutes 'quality' and a multidisciplinary approach to testing that involves user experience design, psychology, and even marketing principles.

Moreover, as the complexity of software systems increases, the demand for specialised testing skills is likely to grow. However, this specialisation should not occur in isolation. Instead, the future test manager must strike a balance, fostering a team that has deep knowledge in specific areas but can also collaborate effectively to ensure a holistic understanding of the system under test.

Another significant trend is the proliferation of big data. The ability to gather, analyse, and derive insights from vast quantities of data can significantly enhance testing efforts. Test managers must, therefore, familiarise themselves with data analysis techniques and tools and learn how to apply data-driven strategies to testing.

Lastly, the ethical aspect of testing is set to take centre stage. With technology infiltrating all aspects of life, ensuring the ethical use of software is becoming crucial. Test managers will need to consider ethical implications such as data privacy, accessibility, and bias in their testing strategies.

Preparing for these future trends involves a proactive mindset. It means continuously learning, adapting, and evolving. It means viewing every change not as a challenge but as an opportunity to enhance the effectiveness and value of testing. By doing so, test managers can ensure that they not only keep pace with the changes but also leverage them to elevate the role of testing in software development.

Conclusion

As we reach the conclusion of this comprehensive guide, it's evident that the role of a test manager is nuanced and multi-faceted. The chapters above have taken us on an extensive journey, exploring a wide range of concepts, responsibilities, and skills that form the foundation of successful test management.

We started by setting the stage with an understanding of the role of the test manager, followed by outlining the crucial process of test planning and test strategy development. As we progressed, we explored the intricacies of overseeing test case design, data management, and environment setup, thereby highlighting the detailed-oriented nature of test management.

The subsequent chapters painted a vivid picture of the actual execution of the testing process. We covered the spectrum of activities from test execution to issue management, and reporting, revealing the dynamic nature of test management. An understanding of quality assurance and control underpinned these processes, emphasising the essential role of quality in all aspects of testing.

Further, we ventured into the exciting world of test automation, exploring its numerous benefits, potential pitfalls, and strategies for effective implementation. This paved the way for a discussion on stakeholder communication and reporting, spotlighting the importance of interpersonal skills in the role of a test manager.

As we delved into the topic of continuous improvement, we underscored the need for test managers to continually evolve and adapt, both in their personal growth and in the processes they oversee. This theme of evolution continued as we explored the development of leadership skills, the promotion of professional growth within the team, and the importance of networking.

In the concluding chapters, we dived into the intricacies of tools and technologies used in test management, providing an overview of popular tools and guidelines for their evaluation and implementation. We also looked towards the future of test management, outlining emerging trends and technologies, and discussing strategies to navigate these new waters.

While this book is comprehensive, it should be viewed as a launchpad rather than a destination. The ever-evolving nature of the technology world means that new challenges and opportunities are continually emerging, and the successful test manager is one who remains committed to lifelong learning and improvement.

The world of test management is as dynamic as it is challenging, but it is also rewarding. It's an opportunity to influence the quality of products that could potentially touch the lives of millions. The best practices and knowledge shared in these pages will provide you with the tools to succeed, but it is your creativity, dedication, and passion for excellence that will truly enable you to make a difference in this field.

This journey that we have embarked on together through these chapters has been engaging and insightful, and I hope that it has provided you with significant value. It is my earnest hope that this book has served as a useful companion to you in your test management journey, regardless of whether you're just starting or are a seasoned professional seeking to broaden your horizons.

If you found this book beneficial, I would deeply appreciate if you could take a few minutes to leave a review on Amazon. Reviews not only help potential readers make informed decisions but also provide invaluable feedback that can be used to improve future editions of the book. I am eager to hear your thoughts, suggestions, and experiences related to the content of this book.

Thank you for accompanying me on this journey. As you progress in your test management career, may you continue to embrace learning, demonstrate leadership, and above all, strive for quality in all your endeavours. Happy testing!